The Meaning of the West

The Meaning of the West

*An Apologia for
Secular Christianity*

Don Cupitt

scm press

Scripture quotations are mostly from the New Revised
Standard Version of the Bible, copyright 1989 by the
Division of Christian Education of the National Council of
the Churches of Christ in the USA. Used by permission. All
rights reserved.

The principal Hebrew Bible passages are from the Revised
Standard Version of the Bible, copyright 1946, 1952 and
1971 by the Division of Christian Education of the National
Council of the Churches of Christ in the USA. Used by
permission. All rights reserved.

British Library Cataloguing in Publication data

A catalogue record for this book is available
from the British Library

978 0 334 04202 0

First published in 2008 by SCM Press
13–17 Long Lane,
London EC1A 9PN

www.scm-canterburypress.co.uk

SCM Press is a division of
SCM-Canterbury Press Ltd

Typeset by Regent Typesetting, London
Printed and bound in Great Britain by
CPI William Clowes Ltd, Beccles, NR34 7TL

Contents

Preface

How should Western culture define itself? What are the core values to which the member states of the European Union are committed? There has been some controversy recently between those who wish to answer such questions in secular, Enlightenment terms (liberal democracy, the rule of law, freedom and individual human rights), and those who see Western culture as being rooted in the Christian and Jewish religions. I begin this book by arguing that the unique dynamism of the West – its fast-growing, science-based industrial civilization, its intellectual energy, and its liberal humanitarian ethics – is at every point dependent upon the West's greatest invention, the 'critical' type of thinking, which in turn is Christian in its origin and inspiration. For example, the liberal-democratic kind of society that we have today, and which is uniquely creative because it is continuously self-criticizing and self-reforming, derives from the older ideas that the Church is (or should be) that kind of society – *Ecclesia semper reformanda* – and that the committed individual believer should be that kind of person.

At this point a second line of argument emerges. If the modern West is the child of Christianity, it is surely a very late offspring, born only from its mother's death. Since about 1750 Christianity the religion, the Christian Church, has been slowly dying. How ironical that the greatest achievements of Christianity – the emergence of the first large-scale free societies in which most human beings, and not just the leading groups, can enjoy a full span of life in good health, peace and prosperity, along with a number of unique moral

vii

achievements such as the emancipation of women – all this, which derives from the ancient biblical dream of a better world, has actually come about only in the period of the terminal decline of religion. It seems that Christian self-criticism, by undermining metaphysical philosophy and the authority of both the Bible and the Church, has liberated and democratized the West to the point where, in the welfare state, the Corporal Works of Mercy are now public policy. Strange: in the so-called 'ages of faith' the state was very cruel; but now, after Christianity, the state has become startlingly Christian. It cares for all.

This paradox prompts me to develop the second line of argument, which is that we should give up thinking of Christianity as being merely a religion, and one of 'the world religions'. Instead we should begin to think of Christianity as a utopian cultural movement, which, emerging as and when it did, had in the short term to take the form of a religion, but which eventually burst out of its religious chrysalis and became the modern world.

The original Jesus remains historically controversial, but there is at least a case for saying that he was a Jewish teacher in the tradition of prophets like Jeremiah. He was critical of organized religion and tradition, and seems to have had little fresh to say either about God, or about sin and redemption. Instead, his chief concern was to convey a utopian vision of what human life could, should, and perhaps soon would, be. However, the ancient Graeco-Roman world was a harsh slave society, and after Jesus' execution it was clear that there was little chance of any early realization of his dream. So he was seen as waiting in the heavenly world, from which he would one day return to earth to establish his Kingdom. The utopian vision was thus deferred, projected into the heavenly world and the far future, and Christianity slowly developed into a religion of eternal salvation from sin at the end of time. An officer-class of professional clergy maintained order among the waiting faithful during the interim period.

The Church gradually became very authoritarian and other-worldly in its orientation. But its language and its historical drive continued to seek its own self-secularization. 'Thy Kingdom come, on earth as it is in heaven', said the Lord's Prayer, and the Church's doctrine continued to speak of God as 'becoming man', and of God's Spirit as becoming diffused through the human world. Many religions include myths which declare that in the original Golden Age the heavenly and earthly worlds were one, but that as a result of some disaster the heavenly world withdrew from earth. Christianity more than any other faith seeks to regain Paradise by bringing heaven back down to this earth and so re-unifying the two worlds. As during the later Middle Ages West European Christians began to develop a richer and more humanistic urban culture, Christianity began at last to seek its own full self-secularization. In all the major phases of cultural expansion that followed in the next four or five centuries (around AD 1300–1800) we see the original utopian and this-worldly humanism bursting out of its stiff religious shell. Woman and domestic life; dress and fashion; printing, and literature for the laity; travel, trade and exploration; Protestantism and the discovery of individual subjectivity; the Enlightenment and an explosion of new knowledge; Romanticism; the democratic revolutions and the industrial revolution; liberal democracy and the rule of law, socialism and feminism – in all this we see the huge energy of the modern world exploding out of the constricting religion-based civilization that had preceded it; or, better (as I would say), we see the original utopian religious humanism coming back down to earth and realizing itself at last. Instead of the old medieval universe of heaven, earth and hell, everything, but *everything*, eventually becomes internal to our human *history*, our human world of *life*, our human world of *language*. And this radical-humanist world – the world of everyday life, the world of the novel – is simply Christianity itself realized, or objectified. God has, at last, fully become human and *only* human.

For many years I laboured to reconcile Church-Christianity and the modern world. I now see that the critics were right, and it cannot be done. Church-Christianity is gradually becoming more and more counter-cultural (a euphemism for 'irrational') and reactionary as it declines. But now I ask: Why *try* to save the Church? It has been historically obsolete for about two centuries. We should let it go, and instead learn to see in modern Western culture itself the human *and Christian* values that we will need to proclaim and defend in the future. As we do this, we develop a new 'secular Christian apologetics'. We discard the institutional side of Christianity, authoritarian and power-hungry, with its supernatural doctrines, and instead we follow out the historical development of Christian spirituality and ethics.

Don Cupitt
Cambridge
July 2008

I

What is the West?

Around the world, people everywhere speak of something they call 'the West'. They love it, they envy and resent it, they want to blame it for almost everything, they want to rival it, they want by any means to get into it, and they are ready to beg, borrow or steal all they can possibly extract from it. They lust after its money. But what is it?

The term 'the West' has been used in this rather obsessive way for only 30–40 years. Before then people spoke more often about 'the developed countries' of 'the First World' as distinct from 'the Second World' (which presumably no longer exists), and 'the developing countries' of 'the Third World'. Before that again, people might simply have spoken of 'Europe', meaning thereby Latin or Western Europe. Around 1860–1960, the phrase 'Western civilization' was popular. Churchill still used it, but he was surely one of the last to do so.

Today we need to distinguish between the old West and the new late-modern or postmodern West. The old West lasted roughly from Julius Caesar to the French Revolution. It was a European cultural order dominated in philosophy by Plato, in religion by the ethical monotheism of the Hebrew Bible, and in law and social organization by the legacy of ancient Rome. The Latin Christian Church was its central and most durable institution. The old West was deeply affected by the rise of modern critical thinking and the Enlightenment, and then during the nineteenth century it entered a period of very rapid intellectual and industrial development. All its founding ideas were criticized by a line of great philosophers, mostly Germans. This violent upheaval culminated in the two terrible World Wars of the early twentieth century, and then, amid an unprecedented surge in prosperity and in world population, the new West led by the USA, that which people now call just 'the West', emerged almost fully developed during the 1950s. Yet, somehow, it is still growing and changing rapidly.

This new West is something like a culmination of human history hitherto, for it is marked by the appearance of the first fully emancipated human beings – people who know themselves to be the only makers of their own world-view, knowledge-systems, technologies and values. Their world is purely human and secular. Their politics is liberal-democratic, their economic order is 'social market' or 'guided capitalist', and their ethic is above all humanitarian. They pay lip-service, at least, to the old ideals of the French Revolution, 'liberty, equality, fraternity', but they freely confess that the realization of these ideals in the social life of Western countries still remains very incomplete. In art and selfhood Westerners are typically Romantics who insist upon seeing themselves as the authors of their own lives, and who love 'fashion' and self-expression. Everyone wants to become him- or herself and to live his or her own 'lifestyle'. These people are highly urban, and their cultural life is a whirl of stories and images. Their outlook is non-metaphysical, consumerist and entirely 'immanent' or this-worldly, so that the place of religion in their lives is now taken just by an intense, quasi-religious love of life and the assiduous cultivation of life-skills. Instead of the 'spiritual director' of former days, they employ such new guides as a 'life-coach'. You could say that their religion is their culture, and vice versa, that their culture is their religion. At one time God or tradition gave us everything: then we decided that we made culture and God gave us religion; and then most recently we have realized that we made everything. Religion and culture are continuous, and they both evolve together. Both are now life-centred.

The old-Western type of religion, of the sort that makes sharp distinctions between things human and things divine, between time and eternity, and between this world and a Better World Above, still survives in the modern West, and of course freely denounces the West for being hedonistic, materialistic, undisciplined, morally relativistic, and all the rest of it; but these mindless denunciations make not the slightest difference to the fact that everybody who can possibly do so wants to get into the West and to become part of it. In this respect the West is like a great supermarket. Of course everybody professes to disapprove of and dislike supermarkets, and deplores the loss of the old high street lined with separate specialist shops dealing in bread, fish, meat, vegetables and so on; but this popular talk does not in any way alter the fact that we will all of us continue unstoppably to flock into supermarkets. A big supermarket stocks 12,000 product 'lines': who complains about having so much choice? And so it is with the West: however much people profess to deplore it, its cultural dominance remains without any effective challenge. Even those whose hatred of the West is most fierce have no alternative but to borrow from it the means – the money and the technologies – with which they will be enabled to fight it. In this sense, even Osama bin Laden is still a Westerner. Of course he is, and so are we all.

But what *is* the West; what is this strange new cultural order which dominates the world, which most people in some degree profess to deplore, and yet to which every single one of us is irresistibly attracted?

The traditionally religious may declare that the West, the new West, is nothing but 'godless materialism', and that everybody who is caught up in it ought to be, and probably is, haunted by horror at the meaninglessness of his or her own life; but this cliché is belied by the fact that we all of us love the West so much. People in the West are about ten times more wealthy than the rest of humanity, have a much longer life-expectancy, and have huge cultural wealth at their fingertips every day. Western society is much kinder to its own weaker members than any previous society ever was. What's wrong with all that?

An alternative, a simpler and a more rational answer to the question about what the West is would be to say that the West is simply the culture-area in which the whole social system, by cleverly combining engineering with capitalism, motivates people continuously to strive to do everything more and more efficiently. Quite early on, we learnt to organize research and the accumulation and application of knowledge; and we have slowly learnt to organize and to safeguard by law the generation, the accumulation and investment, and to some degree the distribution, of wealth. We know how to invest in, and how to maintain, what is nowadays called 'the infrastructure' of a developed country. The astounding achievements of the modern West all depend upon the West's great range of management skills. 'Logistics' is the watchword: we now see the huge value to society of such skills, but they have never been in abundant supply. In the past, and in other cultures, society has always been run by a miscellany of holy men, military captains, land-owners, and kings and their counsellors – an inefficient lot, few of whom clearly understood the almost limitless potential of simply getting and remaining really well organized.

Just social discipline, just being efficient, has huge power to create and to apply knowledge, and so to generate wealth; but what has persuaded people to accept the necessary systems of regulation? Various factors are required: there needs to be a long tradition of the regulation of life by religious law, such as in the old West was found in the monastic order and the canonical hours.[1] The timetabling of life began with the hours of prayer. Next, there needs to be a tradition of belief in a cosmos, a stable, law-abiding and intelligible natural world around us, whose workings we human beings are able to understand and in some degree to manage. In the West this need has been supplied by the doctrine of the creation and preservation of the world by God and for the sake of humanity. Third, there needs to be belief in the working-out of a historical redemption, a progressive liberation of human beings by a long-sustained communal effort over time, such as was given to us in the West by our idea of a disciplined long march together through history towards our final salvation. Fourth and finally, there needs to be an intense interest in ordinary secular human life and the drama of human relationships, of the sort that for us begins, perhaps with Dante or perhaps much earlier, with the secular-humanist fictional narratives of the Hebrew Bible.[2] There needs to be belief that ordinary life is *interesting*, and a strong desire to enrich it.

My thesis is emerging, and you will gather that I disagree with the common view that the development of the modern West depended crucially upon the heritage of Greek culture that was preserved by the Byzantines and the Arabs, and was brought to Western Europe usually via Venice, and mainly after the Fourth Crusade. There are many reasons for objecting to this story. For example, if the new material was so vital, why had it not already brought about the take-off into modernity either in Byzantium or in Islam? Second, the modern West has taken shape, not through the stimulus of, but rather by a struggle *to get away from*, the suffocating influence first of Aristotle (after 1600) and then of Plato (after 1800). The rise of modern science in the West was the result of a successful battle against Aristotle, fought chiefly by Galileo, and the end of metaphysics in the modern West is the outcome of a long guerrilla war against Plato, fought by the philosophers from Hegel to Derrida. And third, is it not arguable that the early 'experimental philosophers', or scientists, of the West owed most not to any of the Greeks, but to Lucretius, a Latin writer who – at least, in principle – was always available in the West?

The fourth argument is the killer. Both in Byzantium and in Islam there was a strong tendency towards some form of Caesaropapism, in which the religious leadership and the

5

political leadership coincide and become absolute in a way that leaves very little space for secular reason and a secular sphere of life. This mistake was not made in the West, which always preserved a secular sphere of life in which autonomous human reason was considered to be sufficient. The West never wholly lost the possibility of naturalistic thinking and dialectical thinking, for before Spinoza there was Erigena (c. 810–77), and before Erasmus there was Abailard (1077–1142). The West preserved secular love poetry and the idea of Woman, and the West always had the stronger sense of history.

So I conclude that it was above all the Judaeo-Christian tradition, in its old-Western version, that supplied the necessary background conditions that have made possible the emergence of the modern West. From Christian doctrine, from the Bible and from the West's coenobitic monasteries we drew the belief in the government of all life, all reality, by a knowable and universal divine Law, and in particular the belief in a stable rationally ordered world of Nature, whose workings we were created able to understand, and partially to control. From the Bible and Christian doctrine we got our interest in understanding the human heart and the drama of human relationships, and our hope for a gradual betterment of ordinary secular human life – a salvation worked out in history. We learnt the importance of 'self-examination' and the rational planning of one's own life. In short, I am suggesting that the emergent 'West' is simply Christianity itself. It has completed its 'historical', disciplinary and ecclesiastical period and is now coming into its fulfilment. What remains of the Church continues to bear witness to yesterday's Christianity, but we don't need it any more, because tomorrow's Christianity is coming to flower so rapidly in the secular conversation of the modern West. Christianity is the religion in which God himself is a secular humanist: he becomes human in the world. Notice the contrast: Islam likes certainty, and is convinced of its own right to establish the rule of divine Law over all of human life. It

has no respect for the secular; whereas Christian.
cially in the West – always allowed and respected the
omy of the secular sphere of life. Christianity is the reli
that acts as a bridge, by means of which humans cross over
from the religion-based civilizations of the past to the new
type of civilization that is now emerging, with its immediate
religion of 'life' and its passionate love of the passing show
of existence.[3] If it was enough for God to be a mere mortal
human in the human world, it should be enough for you.

The modern West, I am arguing, is the legacy of Christianity, and in particular of two central doctrines: the *creation*
and preservation of the world by God, and the final, defini-
tive *incarnation* of God in the man Jesus Christ. In these
two doctrines we see the transfer from God to human beings
of God's own power to impose language upon the chaos of
experience, and so create an ordered, law-governed world;
and also the transfer from God to us humans of the power
to give the world (and each other) value just by the way we
love the world, pour ourselves out into it, and die. Thus
the central Christian doctrines have functioned to liberate
and empower human beings, and so to produce the secular
modern Western world. In the nineteenth century this process was called 'the building of the Kingdom of God upon
earth', and it completes the historical task of religion.

An interesting and important disagreement has now
emerged. Two great faith traditions each claim today to be
simply the achieved reign or 'Kingdom' of God on earth. But
they are in marked contrast with each other. Islam is a faith
younger than Christianity and in some respects much more
rational. It seeks to realize on earth a vision of all reality,
natural and human, as governed by divine Law; but it is notably more determinedly theocentric and much less humanistic than Christianity, and it simply cannot reconcile itself to
the new West. By the reign of God, it really does mean the
reign of *God only*, through sharia, which is God's Law.

By contrast, the Kingdom of God in Christianity is a
purely human world, a world from which God has quietly

and progressively withdrawn. Jesus himself, in the most recent reconstructions of his historical teachings, was an almost purely secular moral teacher. He uses the phrase 'the Kingdom of God', but he has almost no teaching about God as such. Instead, he uses the phrase 'the Kingdom of God' to describe in his parables a purely human life-world such as the prophet Jeremiah describes – a world with no social hierarchy and none of the apparatus of organized religion. People will have the divine Law 'written on their hearts', and will therefore be able to live well by living spontaneously and just *from the heart*. In the Kingdom of Heaven there are no external authorities and there is no God out there.[4] Everything simply flows out from 'the human heart by which we live'. The centuries of life under sacred Law are succeeded at last by an age of pure freedom.

In this vision, originally launched by Jesus himself, the story of salvation is the story of a God who liberates humankind by a progressive kenosis or self-emptying. He disappears into humanity, into the human heart. The Italian philosopher Gianni Vattimo interestingly interweaves here the Christian salvation-narrative with Heidegger's story of the long 'weakening of Being'.[5] Originally, the structures of Being were very strong indeed, and humans were nothing. Objective reality seemed to be overwhelmingly powerful, and human beings to be utterly powerless. Then Being manifested itself as God and created humans; but by doing this God had already begun to delegate something of his own world-naming and world-ordering power and his own power of choice to *us*, and the whole history of salvation thereafter becomes a story of divine kenosis as the old objective God progressively pours himself out into us and fades away. God manifests himself again as the system of religious Law which humans must adopt, interpret and apply. God then gives himself over to history, to contingency and death, by becoming man in Christ. God pours himself out into the human community as the life-giving spirit of love. Finally, the Kingdom of God has come when human beings are fully emancipated and empowered, the age of metaphysics is over, and God remains only as pure Love. Being is now weak and everything has become a matter of interpretation – that is, is mediated by language and history. There is no longer any purely objective Reality to which we must bow: nihilism is our spiritual liberation. Outsidelessly, our human world is now the only world.

Even in the Bible itself this progressive withdrawal of God is already obvious. God is vividly and personally present, as an agent in the narrative, only in Genesis and Exodus. Thereafter he pulls back and hides himself behind his revelation in the Torah, in the prophetic oracles, and in occasional religious experiences. In the New Testament Jesus Christ is in the foreground, and God is heard only as a heavenly Voice speaking from offstage, as at the baptism and the transfiguration of Christ. Sometimes God rattles the scenery, as at Christ's death; but it is very noticeable that in the New Testament as a whole, which is supposedly God's final self-disclosure, God has almost totally disappeared and only Jesus Christ is seen. And Jesus is but a mortal man who dies. So the final revelation of God is simply the Death of God which sets us free, and the Christian atheist reading of Christianity, as developed in the Lutheran tradition by Hegel and others, is correct. The old God of power has become the new God of Love. Universal, non-objective, *human* love.

The two versions of the Kingdom of God on earth now stand forth in stark contrast. The Islamist version remains strictly God-centred, disciplinarian and oriented towards death and a longed-for posthumous blessedness. In Christianity, Calvinism comes perhaps nearest to following the Islamic model. Otherwise, the Christian account is dominated by the idea of love as immediate and heedless self-giving, or self-dissemination. Religion becomes radical humanist, this-worldly and expressivist. The Islamist loves death, but the Westerner loves life. The Islamist sees life as a long march towards salvation on the far side of death, but the Westerner sees life as a dance and finds salvation in solar living – ecstatic, expressive joy in outsideless human life.

In short, the modern West is Christian, not post-Christian but radically Christian, and that is why Islamists hate it so much and must commit themselves to fighting against it – at least, for so long as modern Islam remains dominated by an extreme puritan interpretation of its own tradition.

In parenthesis, the conflict between the God-centred vision (disciplinarian, and oriented towards death and heavenly blessedness) and the human-centred vision (emphasizing spontaneity and freedom, and oriented towards Christ, towards life and love) quite often becomes apparent within Christianity itself. For example, the first millennium was God-centred, whereas the second millennium became increasingly Christ-centred. Eastern Christianity has remained more oriented towards God and the eternal world, whereas Western Christianity has always been oriented more towards time, history and the lived human life and teaching of Jesus. But of course I am saying that in the modern West one of these visions has come true, and is now actually embodied in the whole culture. By dying as 'organized religion' Christianity has finally realized itself as culture. We are all of us radical Christian humanists nowadays, whose religion is approximately that of the 1960s in general, and of W. H. Auden and the Beatles in particular. Our pervasive emphasis on 'lifestyle', our humanitarian ethics, our aid budgets and our political correctness are straightforward continuations of Christian ethics, and none of this is likely to change. One side of the argument has won: in the traditional language of theology, Christ has returned and the Church is obsolete (though, as Dostoyevsky foresaw, the Grand Inquisitor is far from pleased; he loves the Church and spiritual power *much* more than he ever loved Christ).

This suggestion will be controversial; but if it is true that the whole culture has now become radical Christian, then it is not surprising that the Church should have lost its old

moral leadership so quickly. At the beginning of the nineteenth century Hegel could still regard Protestant Christianity as a very important progressive force in society. And in a
sense this was obviously true: great and heroic figures such
as (in England) Clarkson[6] and Wilberforce, the members of
the Clapham Sect, Hannah More and many others were still
battling in the traditional way to better the lives of slaves, of
industrial workers, and of women and children. The state
had not yet become humanitarian: it was not yet generally
seen as having chief responsibility for the good health, the
living and employment conditions, the education and the
general well-being of the 'broad masses' of the population.
The ruling class just *ruled*, and it was still up to people from
the 'Church' side of the culture to come forward and voluntarily to perform corporal works of mercy for the betterment of the lives of the poor. For almost a millennium individual members of the ruling class (including, of course,
kings) had done exactly that when they founded and endowed schools, almshouses, hospitals, colleges and hospices
for veteran sailors and soldiers. In the early nineteenth century this great and noble tradition still continued; but men
like Clarkson and Wilberforce were not merely doing good
locally. They were battling to change not just individual
human hearts, but *the law of the land* at a time when Hegel
was already formulating the novel idea of the 'ethical state',
'der Gang Gottes in der Welt' as he puts it.[7] In the emergent modern West the state was gradually persuaded not
only to make the slave trade illegal under the English flag,
but also to use the Royal Navy to enforce a humanitarian
foreign policy upon the high seas. The state was gradually
persuaded not merely to recognize trades unions, but even
to accept them as being something like one of the estates
of the realm. In short, the state itself has gradually become
actively humanitarian. So is the United Nations, and so indeed is the European Union. And not only does the state
now uses its tax-raising power to care for the unemployed,
the poor and the sick, and to educate children, much more

efficiently and comprehensively than the old voluntary and faith-based system could ever achieve, but also the state to-day is ethically well ahead of the Church – for example, in its readiness to grant full and equal social rights to women, to homosexual people and to its own employees. In these respects civil society is now much more Christian than the Church.

So is not the Church obsolete now? We may point out that it is in many ways convenient that the Church should still be around, determinedly preaching yesterday's now-outdated form of Christianity, because its being there use-fully reminds us of who we are and of the long story of how we got to where we are. (The story, indeed, that I am here telling.) But I am very embarrassed by the present-day Church's ugly moral backwardness. Surely the state must at the very least disestablish it where it remains socially 'estab-lished', and quietly squeeze it in order to encourage it to get its own behaviour up-to-date? As we all of us often say, there must be limits to multiculturalism: that is, there must be limits to the extent to which the state can tolerate im-moralities because they are 'traditional' in some religion or other. Indeed: and that includes *our own* religion.

Our main line of argument has led us through the import-ant contrast between Islamic and Christian interpretations of the evocative phrase 'the Kingdom of God on earth'. For Muslims, Islam is itself the Reign of God: it is a world ruled by the one revealed divine Law, in which all Muslims are citizens of a single Islamic state, the Caliphate. (The historical *calif* was the successor of Muhammad, rather as the pope is the successor to Peter. He ruled in Baghdad till 1258, in Egypt till 1517, and then (in the form of the Ottoman Emperor) in Istanbul till 1924.) For Muslims the Kingdom of God on earth has to be a monarchy, and a few late-medieval Christians such as Dante similarly hoped that their own faith might one day prevail in a Roman World Empire; but the best modern Christian example of the idea of the Kingdom of God on earth pictures it as being very definitely a liberal-democratic republic, the ideal 'America'. We are not talking about Byzantine emperors, Holy Roman emperors, or kaisers or tsars. We are talking about the American attempt to build an earthly society that would be the Kingdom of God because in it human beings would be more completely *freed*, or 'saved', than they had ever been before, anywhere. And in this fully free society there would be complete religious freedom coupled with complete separation of church and state, because the pioneers of America understood very well that if human beings are ever to be fully emancipated then they must above all be emancipated not merely from *political* tyranny but even more, from *religious* tyranny. Thus the free society has to be a secular society of common people living a common life, without any sacred Authority ruling over them other than the laws that they themselves have enacted, laws that give them their freedom.[8]

That dream of pure religious freedom may seem to have become badly tarnished, and perhaps even to be lost altogether by now, but recent developments may be helping to give it a new lease of life. In religion and philosophy there is a perennial dispute between two parties. There are those who think that our greatest need in life is to gain security and blessedness by attaching ourselves permanently and securely to something very much greater, stabler and more perfect than ourselves, sometime that transcends the passing show of existence. I'll call these people the party of metaphysics. They are philosophical realists, for whom our salvation depends upon our relation to something Big out there. The other party includes all those who think that our chief need is to be cured of the errors and discontents that rob us of our ability to enjoy life and live it to the full. I'll call these people pragmatists, or even nihilists. They say that we don't need to attach ourselves to some great big saving Fact out there; we just need deliverance from our own anxieties, our illusions and our self-concern. We just need pure freedom and life-skills.

Into the party of metaphysics we can put Plato and traditional adherents of the three 'Abrahamic' religions, and into
the pragmatist group we can put the purest and greatest
teachers of ethical wisdom, including Jesus, the Buddha and
Nietzsche. In this chapter I have been suggesting that in the
modern West the post-metaphysical, non-theistic and radical Christian vision of the Kingdom of God has triumphed.
We are people who are learning to live without absolutes.
We are content to say 'Yes' to our own contingent, historical life in time. We want to learn to love life and to live in
relations of justice and love with our fellow creatures; and
at the end we'll be content to pass away along with everything else.

2

God Secularizes Himself

Imitatio Dei, the imitation of God, is an ancient theme in Christian spirituality, going back to the earliest times. Ignatius of Antioch, martyred in about AD 107, supplies an example of it when, in a passage that one sometimes hears quoted with great relish, he exhorts his fellow bishops to imitate the divine Silence (i.e. for God's sake, shut up).[9] The idea is, roughly, that we should consider God's nature, his moral attributes, his love and his self-emptying in Christ for our sakes, and then learn to take God as our role-model.

So we *should* play God? But ordinary language uses the phrase 'playing God' pejoratively, and something of the same ambivalence is also embedded in Christian language. Is it right either to aim to become God, or even – and more modestly – to aim to be *like* God? By a sudden reversal, lofty mystical language may come to be perceived as dangerously heretical. Nevertheless, in the Sermon on the Mount in St Matthew's Gospel, Jesus is portrayed as saying: 'Be perfect, therefore, as your heavenly Father is perfect.'[10] Few gospel critics would suggest that the line goes back to Jesus himself, but it would not have been attributed to him unless the idea had currency and authority among the early Christians. And no doubt it did, for it was a commonplace of ancient Jewish teaching that the community of God's people on earth ought to reflect in their conduct something of the divine holiness and righteousness.[11]

The idea is taken just a little further in a saying about Christ that in one form or another is common among the theologians of the early Christian Church: 'He became what you are in order that you should become what he is' – or, a shade more strongly again: 'He has taken upon himself everything that you are in order that you may become everything that he is.' His coming down to *your* level has opened the way for you to rise up to *his*. In this connection it was common to quote Psalm 8: God made humans only a little lower in rank than the members of his own heavenly court; but now we who are united with Christ are raised to a *higher* rank than that of the angel-courtiers, a point often made by theologians in connection with the salvation-narrative as a whole. Christ has blazed a trail, by following which we are to ascend to heaven and share his throne. O happy fault (*felix culpa*), which merited such a great redemption! For the whole story speaks of something more than a mere restoration of the *status quo ante*; it shows that the new cosmic status of humankind-fallen-and-redeemed is higher than its previous *un*fallen status.[12] There is even a suggestion here of deification (Greek, *apotheosis* or *theopoiēsis*), which brings us to a curious and rather sensitive point.

The paradox is this: on the one hand a great deal of Christian language clearly does move in the direction of deification. For example, the believer is spoken of as drawing nearer and nearer to God, even to the point of entering into a spiritual marriage with God, or being united with God, or being drowned in the ocean of divine Love. Again, the redemption wrought by Christ is so complete and so fully adequate that the believer becomes of 'one substance with' Christ, as Christ is of one substance with God. And again, the mystic following the introvertive way finds God 'within'; that is, she finds her own being 'transparently grounded'[13] in God. In all such talk it seems clear that the goal of the religious life is one's own deification: but anyone who actually *claims* deification has historically been in dire trouble, like the Muslim mystic Al-Hallaj, who was lynched in AD 922 (= AH 309). To claim deification is blasphemy, for orthodox monotheism always insists that the 'infinite qualitative difference' between God and the finite human soul remains and is unbridgeable. Even in heaven.

Why is that? Why is it that standard religious language both drives towards deification and denies its possibility? The answer is straightforward: orthodox realistic mono-theism invariably depicts the universe as an absolute mon-archy, and insists that this political set-up is not going to change, ever. The Great King above us knows all about us. He created us, and we are utterly dependent upon him. We desperately need to please him and to win his favour. We feel ourselves unworthy to approach him, but fortunately we have a mediator – indeed, a whole great system of media-tion – to bridge the gulf between us and him.

Now the religious community is always controlled by a body of religious professionals, who operate and guarantee the whole system of mediation. These professionals are high priests, and the highest of them all is called the *pontifex maximus*, the great bridgemaker. This Supreme Pontiff is always there, and he guarantees the structural soundness of the great Bridge – the sacramental system – over which the faithful are passing on their way to God. But the faithful must be always *in via*, on the way, crossing: they can never know themselves to have *completed* the crossing, because in the moment that they step off it on the far side, the bridge becomes redundant. The Pontiff and all his hundreds of thousands of priests are out of a job. They'll not be needed any more! They don't want *that*. So they are stuck with the paradoxical dual statement: (i) the whole great Bridge, the sacramental system and the redemption wrought by Christ that it impetrates or actualizes in us, really does work. It is guaranteed to lead us beyond itself and into God over on the far side. But at the same time (ii), you never get there, not while we are around, say the high priests. Indeed, some theologians have taught that there are popes in heaven, still bridging away and so deferring infinitely the final redemp-tion they for ever guarantee, even while the blessed souls around them are actually enjoying it![14]

All of which proves that the standard, church-enforced 'realistic' interpretation of the Christian doctrine system leads to an insoluble contradiction and cannot be true. And by a similar argument all other forms of organized religion can be shown to fall into the same contradiction. Why? Because all forms of organized religion are controlled by religious professionals who can achieve job security for themselves only by making grandiose promises whose final fulfilment must be infinitely deferred. We can call this 'the antinomy of organized religion': it cannot ever bring itself to deliver the final redemption from itself that it promises.

So far we have not found any entirely convincing anticipation of our own position within the main tradition of Christian language, but the next example seems more promising. Everyone who attends to a great deal of Christian speaking and writing will have heard quoted, in one form or another, a text attributed to St Teresa of Avila which says that Christ 'has no other feet to walk on but yours, no other eyes to look through but yours, no other hands to work with but yours', and so on.

As we usually hear this point being made, it really *does* sound like a radical-humanist reading of Christianity. Christ *is* our imitation of him! The history of salvation is the story of a political revolution at cosmic level, as the old Monarch dethrones himself, becomes human-in-the-world, dies and disperses his own sovereignty into his people. The old divine Monarchy thus transforms itself into a modern human democracy. In the process, Being 'weakens'. In the old order there was only one way that everything could be, namely the way that Almighty God eternally willed it to be. Everything and everyone was fixed. Theological determinism was true, and the structures of Being were very strong. But in the new democratic human order, Being is weak, and what people call 'the real world' is merely a transient communal interpretation that their own conversation has briefly imposed upon the outpouring, chaotic flux of the possible. In this new, 'weaker' order we are the only creators of reality and we are the only historical agents. There is no world but *our* world. God really *has* become human, irreversibly. *We* are now the only makers and redeemers of what we now see to be just our own world, as we describe it and redescribe it. So that's what St Teresa meant: Christ, or God, now works in the world only in and through *your* making and remaking of things. God really *has* become human; his whole self-expression, his eternal Word, has become a man in history in such a way that henceforth Christ is all there is of God; and now that Jesus Christ is dead and gone he in turn remains and acts in the world only in and through the lives of his followers. By this route the old divine Monarchy has become the new radical-humanist democracy. And we? We have learnt to imitate God so effectively that we have entirely replaced him, doing now for ourselves what he used to do for us. Thus in the end the imitation of God means the displacement of God. It means becoming human, as God has done.

But how on earth could Teresa of Avila (1515–82) have said such a thing in the middle of Spain's *Siglo de Oro*? I should now say that I have been unable to trace the source of the 'quotation' from which I began, and I now suspect that it is a recent unhistorical fabrication, like the supposed 'Prayer of St Francis' quoted by Margaret Thatcher as she entered 10 Downing Street in 1979. The Prayer of St Francis reeks of the late nineteenth century; and in the same way we can tell that the Saying of St Teresa is really a bit of modern radical theology that by cleverly disguising itself has succeeded in gaining currency among the dopey orthodox. In the past I have myself been known to advocate deceptions of this kind, by way of *seeding* respectable religious discourse with ideas that may one day blow it up.[15]

St Teresa of Avila – or, more likely, the Teresan apocrypha – thus brings us closer to the ideas broached in the previous chapter, and to a thesis unknown in the first millennium that I think begins slowly to surface in the writing of Dante and Petrarch, and in Italian painting of the *Quattrocento*.

The dominance of the monks is coming to an end: attention
is turning to this world, to secular narrative and to human
love. People begin to see that in the past metaphors and
valuations from this world and from human love had been
taken and used to build up the world of religion, and now
the wheel is turning full circle as the whole world of religious devotion begins to return into the human world and
into everyday life.

The return of the sacred into secular human life can be
a slow and difficult process, as the case of Woman shows
most clearly. For over a thousand years woman had been
alienated from herself in order to create the Virgin Mary, a
young woman at the peak of her sexual attractiveness, but
desexualized so that she becomes a tender, devoted, sub-
missive, nurturing Virgin Mother, woman minus her sexual
combativeness and otherness, woman minus her creativity.
And the creation of this idealized, demure, heavenly woman
left men with no very high opinion of the female being
who remained on earth for them. The full reintegration
of woman, sex and spirit, and the idealization of marriage
has taken several centuries and perhaps is not yet achieved
in full. You may quote Coventry Patmore's *The Angel in
the House* (1854–63), but even the Victorians themselves
laughed at it, and a philosopher like the late Richard Rorty
can still say that he looks forward to the time when men
and women can really be friends. Meaning, we are not quite
there yet – seven centuries after Beatrice caught Dante's eye,
and Laura Petrarch's.

Sex is the slowest and most difficult area of all. In other
areas of life the return of the sacred into everyday, this-
worldly life has happened much more quickly. Thus in 1800
the novel English word 'humanitarian' had a theological,
and indeed a christological meaning: it signified someone
whose account of Christ put all the emphasis upon his
human nature and his human sufferings. By the 1840s it
was customary for preachers like the great F. W. Robert-
son to invoke the love and compassion evoked by the sight

of Christ's sufferings upon the cross, and to redirect these feelings towards the hungry, workless, afflicted people in the side streets not far away from his congregation. Today, I hardly need to do more than mention the almost world-wide triumph of humanitarian ethics. It is remarkably new, but almost everywhere people now acknowledge its claims. Even governments acknowledge its claims.

Another example: the bit of Christianity that changed most during the twentieth century was the language and the observances used in connection with death. In 1900 something of the traditional Christian attitude to death still survived: it was one of the Four Last Things and it prompted thoughts of the Last Judgement, heaven and hell. Today few of my readers anywhere have recently attended a funeral service at which the preacher warned people to think about judgement, heaven and hell, and demanded repentance – or indeed, discussed the afterlife of the deceased at all. On the contrary, every modern funeral is life-centred: the completion of a life is marked by fulsome tributes and reminiscences. Death is now merely life's boundary, and an occasion for us to try to give ritual closure to a person's human life. The recent disappearance of any serious belief in life after death indicates that the full return of the supernatural world into this world is now almost accomplished.

As the return of the supernatural world into this world becomes complete, we understand how it is that Christianity doesn't need any supernatural agency to bring about 'the end of the world' and thereby lead the Faith to its destiny; for on the contrary Christianity by its own inner logic precipitates itself beyond itself. Christianity is the religion that for several centuries now has been passing over into radical religious humanism. It is the religion that more than any other takes us beyond the age of religion into the secular and humanistic age that follows. Christianity's central declaration is that God himself is a secular humanist, that is, one who chooses to be simply a man in the human world (Latin: *saeculum*). That's enough for him, and indeed it is in

a sense henceforth all there is for him. And this self-secularization and self-emptying of God was bound to become the
template for our own eventual secularization of our culture
and faith.

In the light of all this, how do we now understand St
Paul's classic statement about what Christ means to his
readers? It runs:

> Let each of you look not to your own interests, but to the
> interests of others. Let the same mind be in you that was
> in Christ Jesus,
>> who, though he was in the form of God,
>>> did not regard equality with God
>>> as something to be exploited,
>> but emptied himself,
>>> taking the form of a slave,
>>> being born in human likeness.
>> And being found in human form
>>> he humbled himself
>>> and became obedient to the point of death –
>>> even death on a cross.
>> Therefore God has highly exalted him ...
>
> (Philippians 2.4ff.)

As always with his doctrinal arias, the context in which
Paul writes these words is ethical (see Philippians 2.3–4 and
2.14ff.) Like religious people the world over, the group at
Philippi are being arrogant, disputatious and touchy, and it
is necessary for the apostle to tell them to 'come off it', as
the phrase goes. But he must go carefully; he must be tact-
ful. So he sings his aria about how Jesus the Christ had come
down off his high horse in the biggest way imaginable, and
is now gloriously rewarded for it. The moral teaching here
is straight out of the central tradition of Jesus' own message – that is, it is part of Q (Matthew 23.12; Luke 14.11;
17.14b): 'all who humble themselves will be exalted.'

So St Paul tries to talk the quarrelsome Philippians into

being a little kinder to each other by singing to them a doctrinal aria about Jesus as a cosmic figure who has temporar-
ily renounced his place in heaven, has been born a man, has
lived among us and suffered an unjust death on the cross,
and now has been exalted to universal lordship.

Why does Paul think that this christological romance will
persuade his readers? At present our ideas about the evolution of Christian doctrine in the first two decades after
Jesus' death are still somewhat hazy. The best guess we
can propose for now says that Jesus himself was an almost
purely secular teacher of wisdom, whose teaching made a
very deep impression upon his immediate circle. At first
they could see his death only as a case of innocent suffering,
nobly borne. But somehow the message and the new way of
life must go on – which meant that, exactly as happened in
the case of the Buddha, Jesus himself must somehow be seen
as going on, and therefore as being a permanent, cosmic
figure. Local theology begins to supply his new symbolic
dress. He is a righteous man, he is a great prophet and mar-
tyr taken up into heaven like Elijah, he is the adopted son
of God, he is the Messiah-designate who will return, he is
the pre-existent heavenly Son of Man figure, he is God's
expressed Word. And so it goes on, the theology developing in exactly the way one would expect at that particular
place and time. But at bottom, all that it is *about* is the
new ethic of mutual love and forbearance. A huge system
of christological doctrine, a whole world-view and system
of religious mediation develops over the next three or four
centuries, and then lasts a thousand years. Gradually the
wheel turns full circle, and in early modernity the process of
demythologizing begins. When it is complete we return into
the simplest ethical problems of human life together, here
and now. And *that* is the return of the original Jesus – that
is, of his message.

We seem to have arrived at a reductionist account of the
imitation of God, the theme from which I began. It appears
that the gods and the whole world of 'the poetical theology'

were in truth only ever a projection. To make the problems of everyday life manageable, we had to think heterologically. We projected the great issues of life and death out in stories about gods, which we then used as templates on which to model our own behaviour. When I was having a fit of the sulks, I got out of it by telling myself a great story about how the eternal Word of God had come down from heaven, become incarnate, and had lived and died among us, and all for love of us. And by all this story-telling we were able to persuade ourselves simply to 'come off it'— at least, we did so until the early or mid-nineteenth century, when our own psychological understanding and general self-knowledge had reached the point where we could give up heterological thinking, and replace all the old myths with new 'interpersonal skills' and the like. Is that, just that, all there is to it?

Not quite, because even today completely demythologized thinking remains too difficult for most people. Take the Genesis story of creation of the world by God. This now has to be read as a story about how we ourselves have made our world. Read it as your own very abridged biography. You began in a state of formlessness and darkness. There was no real world out there yet at all. What began everything was your first use and recognition of a general sign that linked you with an Other. *Fiat lux*, let there be light! With the first motion of a linguistic sign something like a world is lit up. You begin to be aware of yourself, the language-user, of the world, and of the creative power of the Word. As your mastery and active use of language develop the world gets divided up and sorted out. Light and darkness, heaven and earth, land and sea, plants and animals, culminating in the great distinctions: man and woman, good and evil, innocence and experience, until we reach the last great truth of the human condition, namely our expulsion from Eden and the knowledge of death. *You're on your own now.*

So the whole story in Genesis 1—3 is eventually to be read by each one of us *not* as a story about how an objective God created the world, but as a story about how each one of us makes her world, makes herself, and comes gradually into a full understanding of the universal human condition. How could it all be better taught than it is taught by the biblical myths? Even today the true interpretation of the story cannot be preached in church – it would not be allowed – and even today people remain reluctant to recognize the extent to which we construct our world and ourselves within the motion of our language. This is odd, because familiar Romantic poets like Wordsworth made the essential points clear to everyone 200 years ago. But there it is: it is hard to come to terms with some of the most basic truths of life, so hard that many people even today can reach them only via religious myth and the *imitatio Dei*.

The Genesis myths will continue to ring bells (and to be quite independent of scientific theory) for some time yet. But I hope the time will soon come when many people will be ready to live entirely without illusions, and to rejoice in the practice of a purely ethical religion of everyday human life.

3

The West as Secularized
Christianity

As has already been said, Europe – and in particular Latin
or Western Europe – is the ancient heartland of 'the West',
a region whose chief institution has historically been the
Western Church. Its chief bishop, the bishop of Rome, is
traditionally styled 'the Patriarch of the West'.[16] It is well
known that the Latin Church, which in quite recent years
has come to be generally known as 'the Roman Catholic
Church',[17] has always incorporated into its own culture
much of both Greek philosophy and Roman law, as well
as, of course, the Hebrew Bible. It would surely seem then
that what people nowadays call 'the West' is the offspring
of the old West, which in turn more or less coincides with
the culture of the Latin or 'Roman Catholic' Church, a culture that synthesizes the legacy of ancient Israel, Greece
and Rome. From about the fifth to the eleventh centuries
this church's culture was itself almost all that the peoples of
Western Europe had to think with and to live by.[18]

Yet, paradoxically, modern Europe has repudiated this
heritage. Despite the urgent protests of the Vatican, the
European Union recently agreed to define its own 'core values' in purely secular terms (liberal democracy, the rule of
law, human rights, etc.) without any express reference to
religion.

There are some important practical and political reasons for this silence about Europe's Christian past. Modern
Europe is largely secular, and is also multifaith with many

millions of Muslim citizens. Not only has Islam played a large part in the history of several parts of Europe, from Spain to Greece, but also those who favour the admission of Turkey to the EU are very keen to signal to the Islamic world that it is possible for a historically Muslim country to become liberal-democratic and even a welcomed part of 'the West'. We should not at this time be reviving the memory of the religious-territorial blocs of the past, such as 'Christendom' and 'Islam': rather, they say we should strive to build a modern, secular EU within which people of many different faith traditions can coexist peacefully.

This argument sounds at first very reasonable, but it raises one or two questions. It is paradoxical that we should hear so much of it from the French. France is indeed the leading exponent of a secular vision of Europe, but France must surely know how unattractive and even unintelligible secularism is to the Muslims, and how unlikely it is that Muslim Arabs will ever accept the carrying-out of anything like Kemal Ataturk's programme of 'Westernization' within their own traditions. Islam is a highly public faith: it hates the thought of being pushed away into private life. And is not France herself 'the eldest daughter of the Church', and a land in which the spirit of Christian nationalism is even yet not dead?

Today two rather sharply opposed parties dispute over the definition of the West. The secularists follow Gibbon in wanting to bracket out the thousand years of darkness between Augustine and the Italian humanists (400–1400), and thereby to establish a direct connection between the enlightened in antiquity and in modernity. The independent, critical type of thinking and the freedom of speech that it demands have gradually eroded away Tradition and have given us modern critical scholarship, modern liberal-democratic politics, modern science-based industrial society, and our own 'lifestyle' ethics of expressive freedom and human rights. The West has developed a kind of society in which the average person can enjoy a longer, freer and more culturally rich life than any previous human beings have ever had. And the whole self-criticizing, self-developing cultural system that we call 'the West' is secular through and through. Just as Darwinian natural selection must be free from interference in order to deliver the most vigorous results, so the West needs to be secular, an open cultural market, in order to be free to work in the way it does. Anything with authority over it, anything fixed, would inhibit the West's unique capacity for continuous innovation.

On this account the West's peculiar virtue is that it is a continually self-criticizing and self-reforming cultural system which is capable of endless innovation and new possibilities of freedom. But it likes to make a sharp distinction between the secular and the religious, and to reserve the public realm entirely for itself. The bargain is that just about any religion will be tolerated, provided that it understands its place – which is firmly within the private sphere of life. Only 50 years ago, in the USA, there were still public intellectuals who were men of religion, such as Tillich and Niebuhr. Not now: much of the new West is becoming consciously secular and increasingly anti-fundamentalist.

The kind of secularism I have just described is firmly post-Death-of-God. Notice what a lot of systems are now said to work best if they are not in any way planned, or guided from Above: language, democracy, capitalism, biological evolution, and even art. In each case the argument is the same: the way things go should be left to an immanent play of forces, and we must give up the idea that it needs any ultimate Ground, or guiding Hand, or supervising Academy to keep it on the right track. You cannot have and keep real freedom unless you *trust* freedom, and are prepared to live without any authority or certainty.

So much for the secularist idea of what the West is. The alternative idea, which calls itself 'traditionally religious', could hardly be more flatly opposed. It is in a broad sense foundationalist. It declares that experience everywhere shows that human life is meaningless and chaotic unless lived within a guiding framework of objective reality, objective truth and an objective moral law. More than that, we need also a moral Providence, a moral Plan for world history as a whole within which our own lives can find their place. All this is given to us in a uniquely clear, complete and final form within the Western tradition by our ethical monotheism and by the Christian theology of universal history. The core doctrines were first outlined by St Paul, and then classically formulated by St Augustine of Hippo. They were subsequently restated by the Protestant Reformers of the sixteenth century, and remain today as vital as ever.

From this tradition the West gets its conviction that we live within an ordered universe whose laws we humans are intended to discover and exploit. From the same tradition we derive our concepts of the individual human self as a responsible moral agent within its own individual vocation and destiny, and of the larger human community as a mighty army marching through history towards the promised, blessed consummation to which it looks forward. The West's historical dynamism and its worldwide leadership today depend entirely on these doctrines – all of which ultimately come from the biblical revelation.

The truth of all these ideas is certified to us by divine revelation in Scripture, interpreted (as some would add) by Tradition; and, in addition, some will also claim that a number of the central doctrines can also be shown to be true by 'unassisted' human reason. Furthermore, observation of the human scene at large shows that where the Western Christian theology of human existence prevails society flourishes, and where it does not prevail, society stagnates.

It follows, say the religious foundationalists and fundamentalists, that all the core 'Western values' come from the Judaeo-Christian tradition. The West will survive only for so long as it remains faithful to the religion upon which its values depend. Today's secularism threatens to leave the West without the strength to resist its Muslim and other critics.

I have framed the discussion in such a way as to bring out as sharply as possible the conflict between the two opposed accounts of what the West is.

For the liberal nihilists the West is above all critical thinking. The West is at heart an independent, questioning cast of mind for which nothing is entrenched, nothing is sacred, and (conversely) everything is on the table, negotiable, open to reappraisal, revision and reform or reframing. In short, the West is a uniquely vigorous culture based upon a fully open market in ideas.

But to those whom I have long called 'realists', people who belong somewhere on the spectrum that runs from realism/foundationalism to fundamentalism, this liberal nihilism (which they often describe as 'relativism') is a disaster. In postmodernity it has left the West naked and unable to resist its many determined new enemies. The only way to defend Western values is by returning to the core metaphysical and theological beliefs upon which they are founded. The essence is the biblical revelation; or, on the more expanded Catholic account, it is Plato and Aristotle, the Bible and St Augustine, and the Western Church's medieval synthesis. Since about the time of Erasmus, or perhaps even since about the time of William of Ockham (or even perhaps St Bonaventure), mistakes have been made and emergent modernity has mistakenly tried to break away from its Christian foundations. But we must not let it succeed, or we will lose everything that is most precious to us. Somehow the old Ark of Salvation is still just about afloat. We must patch it up and even restore it, if we are to save the West.

It will not have escaped the reader that on my account the conservative religious view of the West more or less identifies the cause of religion with that of realism. For the religious conservative, we haven't got salvation unless we've got mind-independent reality out there, truth out there, and value out there. The conservative is someone for whom meaning must be *inherent*, subsisting out there and independent of our thinking. To live, he must have a fully furnished world all laid on for him. But for the secular liberal 'nihilist' the total freedom of thought and of artistic expression that we love more than anything requires us to suppose that all meanings are *ascribed by us*. We and we alone attribute reality, attribute meanings, truths and values. Our common human life-world is a collective, slowly evolving human construct which is developed and enriched in various ways by scientists, artists, moral reformers, poets, engineers and many others. And what do we build our common world out of? We modify and supplement what we have received from the previous generation. We float new idioms, new evaluations, new images – and some of them stick, to become part of our legacy to those who will come after us. That is culture.

In the present book I am proposing a view that cuts across the conventional distinction between the religious and secular realms. Neither the liberal-nihilist nor the religious conservative account of what the West is and stands for can be accepted quite as it presents itself. The liberal-nihilist story is philosophically very attractive, but unless we can infuse it with religious feeling and symbolism, and so democratize it, it will be far too dry and elitist for the great majority of people. Its nihilism frightens most ordinary folk. The number of thinkers, artists and other creative people who are passionately committed to pure freedom of thought and expression is small, and will perhaps always remain so. Religion will be needed if the artists are to get the masses onto their side, and in support of what they are doing.

As for the conservative-religious story about the Christian origins of Western values, it ignores the well-known historical fact that many or most of our cherished Western values of freedom, toleration and so forth were forged through a long and very harsh struggle *against* an overwhelmingly powerful and ruthless religious dictatorship of the Church, whether Catholic or Protestant. Organized religion with its fixated love of power has, as often as not, been the bitterest enemy of human intellectual, moral and expressive freedom.

Let us make the point more precisely. Just as within the corpus of Plato's writings we find the origins of *both* the questioning *and* the dogmatic-metaphysical traditions within Western philosophy, so in a very similar way we find within the Hebrew Bible the origins *both* of God's absolute monarchy over the human soul *and* of an indestructible human urge to question God's justice and argue with God even to his Face. The great merit of the Western tradition is not that it has always been a coherent set of absolutely splendid ideas, but that from the very beginning in religion, in philosophy and in social ethics, our tradition has always been a running argument, and always somewhat at odds with itself. The great polarities – order versus freedom, rationalism versus voluntarism, realism versus nominalism, loyalism versus dissent, love versus justice – go on for ever. Notoriously, many of the greatest 'saints' in the Western religious tradition went through lengthy periods of the blackest despair (and often in their later years). The strength of the West has always lain in its extreme restlessness, its incipient scepticism and its inability to settle down for long.[19]

My thesis, then, is that the Judaeo-Christian tradition has always been many-stranded, argumentative and somewhat at odds with itself. The great theological themes of God's special purpose in creating humans, his self-revelation to them, his providential guidance of their collective history towards a final consummation, and, above all, his incarnation in Jesus Christ – all these themes together, critically examined and argued over, have made Christianity a uniquely self-secularizing faith. God takes the initiative, moving towards humanity, giving himself to humanity, becoming human and dying *into* humanity. In the end, as St Paul puts it, 'all things are yours'.[20] The entire supernatural order communicates itself to us, and passes away into the human world. God is a secular humanist, content to become just a mortal in the human world and to die. All the old 'absolutes' disappear, except for God's shade, which is simply Love.

In the modern West, then, we live in transition between two versions of Christianity – the old ecclesiastical version which came to its natural end during the early nineteenth century and is now slowly passing away, and our late-modern or postmodern civil society, which is the new 'Kingdom' version of Christianity now becoming firmly settled in. Liberal-democratic civil society is, if you like, Quakerism writ large. It is Christianity at last becoming completely and purely this-worldly and human. It has outgrown hierarchy (the old, ugly, government of the *laos*, the people, by an officer-class of religious professionals, the clerics who control everything), and therewith has outgrown the division of the world into two realms, one sacred and the other profane. Instead there is now only one world, the human world, the world of the novel, which is the typical art form of our secular humanism. The change that has taken place may be seen by comparing the old 'steeple-house' with the Quaker 'meeting house'. The 'steeple-house' – the traditional church building in Quaker parlance – was divided into two zones, the chancel and the nave. In the chancel were the sacred ministers, the performers, the professionals, wearing the white garments of heaven. In the nave, the laity wearing their secular dress participate at one remove in the worship of heaven, hoping to be lifted out of everyday reality for a while. But in the meeting house that division between two realms and two classes of people has simply disappeared. There are no *sacerdotes*, priests, and there is no hierarchizing of reality. Instead, there is only a meeting of friends. The entire divine realm has become scattered or disseminated into human beings.

It is not surprising that the church polity of groups like the Congregationalists, the Independents and the Society of Friends was the historical forerunner of modern secular liberal democracy. Often their buildings, especially in America, were the obvious places to use for the proto-democratic political assembly.

Apart from these points of social organization, the general

picture of the human condition remains in late modernity very strikingly Christian. A famous illustration of the point is the similarity between Rudolf Bultmann's account of St Paul's 'doctrine of man' and his friend Martin Heidegger's account of the human condition in *Being and Time* (1927). Bultmann was a Lutheran, and Heidegger a rather lapsed Catholic. Bultmann had some claim to be the best theologian of the century and Heidegger to be the best philosopher; and the two agreed between themselves to keep their subjects quite distinct. Nevertheless, the similarity is striking, and a vivid reminder to us all that whether we like it or not we are what Christianity has made us.[21]

Even more striking is the extent to which the modern Western-led international ethic is simply a continuation of Christian ethics. The ethic of the UN and the EU, of our international humanitarian organizations, of our civil law and our 'political correctness', is simply left-liberal-Protestant *Christian* ethics, and nothing else.

In short, the modern secular West is simply Christianity in its final, secularized, humanistic, third-millennium, 'Kingdom' form. The clinching realization, at least in a country like Britain, is the realization that civil society, 'secular' culture, is now much more consistently Christian than is the national Church. The Church clings to its old inefficiencies, discriminations and injustices, and repeatedly demands for itself opt-outs from legislation that would require it to get its treatment of its own employees, women, gays and other groups up to decent contemporary secular standards. But by its foot-dragging in these matters the Church demonstrates that its version of Christianity is now obsolete. We should leave it, and instead commit ourselves with full religious seriousness to the best of our contemporary secular cultural life. We'll find the air a great deal more wholesome – and more Christian.

A possible objection that may be raised is this: what of 'nihilistic', unrestricted critical thinking? What of Descartes' method of universal doubt? Can it really be claimed that the West's tradition of radical free thinking is also of Christian origin?

I think it can. Even at the headquarters of Roman Catholicism the usefulness of the role of the *advocatus diaboli* as a tester of evidence and of the strength of arguments has long been freely acknowledged. In addition, it has always been acknowledged that each of us has a devil, or a devil's advocate, in his own head, testing his own faith and encouraging him to doubt God, the presumption here being that every believer who is a thinking person cannot but be aware of the constant presence of an inner gnawing demon of doubt. Thus Christian spirituality has always been aware of the ceaselessly questioning critical spirit, and has also recognized that in some contexts at least that spirit can and should be harnessed and used as the most potent tester of truth known to us.

A further argument is very well known to us from Nietzsche's use of it. From St Paul onwards there was in Christian spirituality something like an infinite demand for intellectual and moral integrity. Believers spent much time in self-examination, trying to be honest with themselves; and Nietzsche of course argues that in the end this quest for inner truthfulness has undermined faith in Christian dogmatic teaching. Here it is sufficient to say that there was from the very beginning a lively tradition of Christian psychology. It owed much to the line in Genesis 6.5 about the *yeser hara*:[22]

> The LORD saw that the wickedness of humankind was great in the earth, and that every inclination of the thoughts of their hearts was only evil continually.

Thus one might say that Christian psychology was already proto-Freudian, and that the believer knew very well how important it was to 'test the spirits', and to be always alert and self-critical.

Along these lines the critical kind of thinking that gives

the modern West its dynamism – and which is often said to lead straight to nihilism – can be seen to have a Christian background. Christian spirituality involved progress in the spiritual life by a continual activity of self-criticism and self-reformation. Nor was this idea found only at the individual level, for there was also a tradition of declaring that the Church too ought to be continuously criticizing and reforming itself. It is somewhat inaccurate to think of the Western Church as *semper eadem*, always the same, and never budging an inch. On the contrary, the Church always knew that vigilant self-criticism is needed to maintain institutional health.

In summary, I stick with the view that the postmodern West is secularized Christianity. Since the Enlightenment a vast number of people have supposed that one can reject Christian dogma and leave the Church – and thereafter have no further connection with Christianity. Not so. We remain what Christianity has made us, and in many respects the postmodern West is more Christian than ever. If you are a Westerner and are committed to Western values, then you are a Christian. A 'crusader-zionist', indeed, says Mr bin Laden indignantly, and he's right again.

4

The Indelible

In hell, says St Augustine, you will find it easy to identify the Christians because they will still have the baptismal mark of the cross on their foreheads. In his own picturesque and slightly malignant way, Augustine is making the technical point that the sacrament of baptism is indelible. Apostates, even when they are damned souls in hell, remain visibly baptized Christians.

Translating this rather mythological idea into our own culture's terms, Augustine's point is that even a lapsed Catholic is still unmistakeably a Catholic, and even the firmest post-Christian is still very definitely a Christian. Even after you have renounced all the Christian supernatural beliefs, and have also severed all your remaining links with the Church, and even if in addition you are conscientiously opposed to many points of standard Christian ethical teaching, there may still be various respects in which you remain indelibly a Christian. For example, if you were raised in Western Europe rather than in Japan, you were raised in a 'guilt culture' rather than a 'shame culture', and this will have made an indelible mark on you.

The point was neatly illustrated two decades or so ago, when the first large mosque was built in Rome and its managing committee invited the members of the Italian parliament to the opening ceremony. Most of the MPs found that they simply could not bear to attend, and they had to decline the invitation. They were very happy to be lapsed, non-practising Catholics in a Catholic country. But they simply could not endure the thought that historical change

37

might be turning them into unbelievers in a Muslim country. If these politicians were people genuinely emancipated from religion, you might expect them to be cheerfully unconcerned about what was going on in the place of worship down the road. But that was not the case at all: a Catholic atheist is a quite different animal from a secular Muslim, and a culture that is historically Latin Christian is very unlike a culture that is historically Muslim, so that those lapsed-Catholic parliamentarians found that they very much needed a strong Catholic Church to go on existing and protecting their lapsed-Catholic identity for them. And indeed we have all heard jokes about the people who define themselves by the Church or synagogue that they *don't* attend.[23] They do: they really do.

We have met another example of the same point already. Martin Heidegger, as we remarked earlier, followed the German Lutheran convention by aiming to keep his philosophy quite independent of theology, and vice versa. Nevertheless, his *Being and Time* (1927) is clearly a product of the main Western Christian 'doctrine of man', and entirely loyal to the great tradition of Paul, Augustine, Luther and Kierkegaard. And Hamlet, and Sartre, one might add. And a few more: Freud, Lacan, Žižek, maybe. It is only too easy to imagine that one has become quite independent of one's own ancestral religious tradition while yet constantly betraying the fact that one still stands firmly within it. For the fact is that much or all of what is most important in Christianity has become so deeply assimilated that we are no longer aware of it, and nobody has yet studied it in any systematic way.

Here is a curious fact: nobody has ever yet even thought of writing *a theology of the indelible* – that is, of all the vital cultural material that is of Christian origin, but which post-Christians find they have not thrown off and cannot throw off. The easiest example is the typically Western form of individual selfhood – selfhood as anxiety and the consciousness of sin; selfhood as a constant nagging awareness of a gap between the self that I know I should be and like to think of myself as being, and the self that is revealed in my actual behaviour; and selfhood as dual, with always a highly comical contrast between the unworldly, idealistic, posturing, ineffectual master-self and the short, rotund, earthy, low-life, cynical, lecherous, evasive servant-self. Don Quixote and Sancho Panza, the Ego and the Id, and so on through dozens of permutations. Always in the West self-consciousness is high, with faint overtones of embarrassment, or guilt, or self-dissatisfaction, and whatever form it takes this awareness of some degree of inner duality and alienation always sets us a problem. Always in the West there is a stronger interest in biography and autobiography than is found anywhere else in the world. We cannot help being self-critical. We want to read about 'the progress of the soul', about 'the growth of the poet's mind', about *Bildung* – about, in short, the human struggle to find some way of forging a unified self, or at least to find some way to mitigate our own chronic self-dissatisfaction. We love life-histories and the dramas of selfhood.

Every person who is of the West has some acquaintance with the matter I have just sketched, whether or not you are still a Christian, whether or not you 'go to church' and assent to the system of supernatural beliefs outlined in the Creed. This view of the self that I am talking about is part of the indelible – and it is of course a thing of purely Christian origin, being derived chiefly from the seventh chapter of St Paul's Epistle to the Romans. It is purely Christian and it is also indelible, because when you have been deeply touched by the mode of consciousness I am talking about you are stuck with it for life, and it will be part of you till your dying day. Paul's writing is good enough to have communicated his form of consciousness like a viral infection to millions of readers, and indeed to a whole great culture.

What else may be reckoned part of the indelible? I believe we must also include here some central themes of Christian ethics, because it seems that if we have ever felt the moral force of these ideas we find ourselves permanently influenced by them, even *after* we have finally broken away from Christian theology and from the Church. They are:

1 The belief in the uniqueness and unique value of each individual human person so that nobody can be lightly written off or regarded as expendable. Everybody should count for one, and nobody for more than one.
2 The ethic of mutual love and forbearance.
3 The principle that the weakest and most vulnerable members of society, who may seem to be riff-raff, still make an unignorable moral claim upon our love and care. We ought to *notice* them and try to do something for them, and that is that.

My suggestion is that once Christianity had imprinted these moral ideas upon the Western mind, they became part of the indelible. We cannot throw them off. They stick with us willy-nilly. Sometimes the rich and powerful affect to be tough, and set their faces against the ethics of equality and humanitarian compassion. Nietzsche notoriously tries to be tough-minded. But I don't believe it, and my counter-example is the well-known fact that every year nowadays there are a large number of humanitarian catastrophes in one part of the world or another, caused by drought, or famine, or war, or simple misgovernment, or other natural disasters – and every year the West funds some sort of charitable relief through UN agencies, or through one or another of the great humanitarian organizations, or by direct subscription. Christian or not, and 'compassion fatigue' or not, we all know that we ought to do something,[24] because once the Christian ethic had been released upon the world, it was sure in the end to become part of the indelible – even for people to whom the idea of God's compassionate outgoing love for humanity no longer means a thing, and even well beyond historically Christian territories. Christian humanitarian ethics has now touched the whole of humanity, and is still working out its full effects.

Another and rather different example is the very wide-spread presumption of 'the uniformity of nature', which leads us to believe that we can build a picture of the world as governed by universal natural laws which are accessible to us, and which give us some chance to develop reliable technologies. Originally this belief was strongly theological. It was associated with the Noachian Covenant (Genesis 8.20—9.17) and with belief in the faithfulness of God.[25] But even after that particular belief has gone, belief in the possibility of natural science and technology has survived and developed. Plato himself was pretty pessimistic, saying that in terms of his view of the world natural science can never be more than 'a likely myth'. Even Aristotle, though much more pro-science, does not claim to deliver any fully *cosmos-wide* natural laws. But biblical theism has left us with an indelible conviction that scientific knowledge and effective technologies based upon it are indeed possible.

A fourth example of the indelible is the belief in progress, which of course has itself progressed considerably. Already within the Bible there is a clear conception of historical development, because the people of God find themselves moving through a series of 'dispensations' as the history of salvation moves forward. Morality changes historically, as for example when the polygamy and concubinage of the Patriarchal Age are succeeded during the period of the Mosaic Law by a presumption of monogamy. In much later times the idea of historical progress itself becomes secularized and humanized, so that we can outline a sequence of stages as follows:

1 A progressive series of dispensations.
2 A progressive history of revelation.
3 A progressive betterment of the human condition by the successive acts of God within human history.
4 A progressive enlightenment of humankind by the growth of knowledge, by free public debate, and by the clarification of consciousness.

5 A progressive *empowerment* of humans by the accumulated development described above.
6 A progressive moral emancipation of humanity and betterment of the human condition by the historical action
   of human beings themselves.

The idea of progress has itself progressed considerably,
and in its development reveals the same gradual transfer
of powers from God to humans that we have already been
talking about – and which, we are arguing, is the hidden
agenda of Christianity itself.

A complication must be briefly disposed of: in the late
nineteenth century a few people (E. Renan, H. G. Wells)
began to put forward the new idea that the main *motor*
of progressive historical change is new developments in science and technology. Science-fiction writers have particularly taken up this idea. But more recently a succession of
environmental panics – overpopulation, resource exhaus-
tion, climate change – have called the belief in progress into
question.

However, this does not affect my general thesis, which
is that the belief in progress is of the indelible sort, for it
always involves a transition from innocence to experience
or from a narrow and 'sectarian' to a much wider form of
consciousness, a transition which is irreversible and therefore indelible. You can't go home again; your former childhood innocence is not recapturable. Similarly, once you
have really believed that it is possible for us humans to make
the future better than the past, you cannot forget the idea
altogether.

The fact that I write these words on Whitsunday 2007
reminds me of a further and dual indelible. Almost from
the very beginning it was decided that membership of the
Church would be open to people of every nation. The faithful were 'elect from *every* nation': God has graciously elected
you to be a Christian, and you for your part were not born
ethnically Christian but had freely chosen your own faith.

The result of all this is that everyone who has been through Christianity is sure to maintain that each of us should be able to regard herself as having freely chosen to be what she is and to believe everything that she does believe. In full; *really* in full. We choose our own being. Second, Christianity commits us permanently to the idea that it is better to be catholic or ecumenical or internationalist in our outlook, rather than to be narrowly ethnocentric.

It cannot for a moment be claimed that historic Christianity has always been true to these principles. There are still persecuting churches, there are still stubbornly ethnocentric national churches, and there are still plenty of small sects. But the ideal has remained, and we are still influenced by it. A fully free person is someone who can see himself as having freely chosen all that he is, believes, values and does, and whose sympathies are not limited by his ethnicity.

I shall not embark here upon the novel and difficult task of trying to describe the whole of the indelible, but the few examples given should be sufficient to illustrate my general contention, which is that the so-called decline of religion, with its presumed corollaries of the eventual disappearance of the Church and of all the Christian supernatural beliefs, does not necessarily mean the end of Christianity. Not at all, because so much of what is most important in Christianity has already become indelible and will probably survive for as long as there are human beings. We cannot unlearn what it has taught us, because it has changed us in an irreversible way. It is still at work, changing us. And what is more, some of these indelible long-term effects of Christianity have now come to be impressed not only upon ex-Christians, but upon all humanity.

A general theological thesis is now beginning to emerge: it is that Christianity is a conscious-raising religion which has always tended in the long run to bring about indelible change in the peoples and cultures that have been deeply affected by it. In some cases the irreversible, 'indelible' change has been very long delayed; but it still happens. The two outstanding examples are the thoroughgoing political and social emancipation of slaves and of women. In both cases the advance of the moral cause in the West has been agonizingly slow and cautious, but in our own time we are at last beginning to see the moral advance in each case both as being indelible once made, and as having been implicit in Christian ethics from the first. At any rate, ambiguous though the Christian record is, the great emancipation movements were launched and were successful in Christian societies *and not elsewhere*.

For example, slavery is taken for granted in the Old Testament, and is not condemned in the New. It was only slowly mitigated by the Christian Roman emperors from Constantine to Justinian. Then it evolved into the serfdom of early medieval Europe. In the sixteenth century slavery was reintroduced into the Americas by European settlers, despite papal condemnations of it. In the eighteenth century the modern Abolitionist movement led by Quakers and Evangelicals appeared, and eventually prevailed after a century of struggles which included many slave revolts and, in the USA, a bitter Civil War. All this is familiar, but we tend to forget that various sorts of bonded labour and 'human trafficking' still flourish today. It is all a very long and chequered history, and it is going to go on for many years yet because economic migrants are now so many, so desperate for work, and so vulnerable to cruel exploitation. Nevertheless I think we can still say that a general conviction of the wrongness of slavery is nowadays 'indelible' among us in the West, inspiring us with the confidence that in the long run every sort of slavery will surely be abolished. Quietly and determinedly we say to ourselves that we are *not* going to give this one up. And something similar has to be said about feminism: once you have really taken in the case for feminism, it tends to become morally indelible in you. It is a cause that in the long run must and will prevail everywhere.

One last example of something very Western, very Christian, which emerges and becomes indelibly impressed only rather late in the development of the Christian tradition, is the very high estimation in which we have come to hold the greatest examples of human creativity. In the first fifteen centuries or so God was the only creator, and human creativity was played down or denied. But the shift of attention from God to man produces at last, in the pages of Giorgio Vasari (1511–74), the beginnings of the modern cult of the artist as 'great'.[26] During the Enlightenment, and especially among the Romantics, the transfer of pure world-shaping creative power from God to the major artist finally becomes quite explicit in the language people commonly use, and by now it has in effect become part of the indelible.

Against this background, the theological thesis I am proposing is that Christianity is the religious movement that, perhaps more than any other, has tended to generate indelible change in the peoples affected by it. The history of Christianity is therefore twofold. The whole story is a story of how world-building and world-changing powers have been gradually transferred from the gods in the supernatural world to human beings in their own life-world, the world of history. And second, as the whole lengthy process continues, it brings about what I am calling indelible changes in human beings as, one after another, new assumptions, new ways of thinking and new valuations become entrenched, irreversible and largely unconscious. If we could give a systematic account of the indelible difference Christianity has already made to humanity, we might be able to estimate how far it has got with its task of achieving human redemption.

Against the background of this twofold history of Christianity, it is clear that we need a larger theory of what Christianity is for human beings, and has done for them so far, than has yet been proposed.

The history of Christianity can scarcely be traced back further than the history of synagogue Judaism – that is, about 23 centuries. But this short time-scale needs to be set in the context of a larger history that reaches back into

Palaeolithic times, when human beings experienced the word as an almost totally unmanageable scrum of powers, and struggled hard to develop even the most elementary cosmology.

In the long run, the desire is (of course) for world control. When humans were desperately weak the only way they could think of formulating a systematic cosmology was by heterological thinking – that is, by imagining super-beings who were free from human weakness, and did have the power to establish an ordered cosmos and thereafter to keep it firmly under control.[27] Such beings were the gods, and theology was from the first a highly heterological style of thinking. It had to be so, because our human weakness was so desperate that we could understand it and imagine an escape from it only by thinking of the world as established and now controlled by very powerful spirits. The god in-directly helped me to understand what I am by being such a potent image of all that I am *not*: only in a rather veiled way was the god *also* an image of what I hope one day to become.

Monotheism pushes this way of thinking to the limit, but when thought reaches something like full ethical mono-theism it also begins to picture God as having graciously handed over something of his world-controlling powers to men. Since at this time men were hunters, and the only bit of world-controlling power that they had was a little bit of control over names, they began picturing God as delegating to men the task of naming the beasts.

God promises that the natural world will be regular and law-abiding, and then gives to humans through a great prophet the system of sacred Law that they are to live by. Thus God gives to humans an orderly cosmology, and there-with some participation in his own knowledge and under-standing of the created order.

Thereafter, as we have already seen, the movement of thought that had projected out an Almighty Creator-God goes into sharp reverse. The 'weakening of Being' is God's steady transfer to humans of his own powers, powers to create reality, order the world, understand and change the world, imagine new things, and create new values. The chief focus of the whole story is the incarnation of God in man in Christ and his death for our sakes; and our AD/BC dating system shows that we still regard God's becoming man as the hinge of world history.

Then in early modern times we see signs that the whole process is approaching completion. In politics, the old absolute monarchy gives place to the new liberal-democratic republic. In metaphysics the old dogmatic realism gives place to a new kind of philosophy, variously called idealism, constructivism, anti-realism or pragmatism, and even nihilism – what is happening being that as more and more is transferred to human beings and internalized, objective 'reality' disappears. With the Death of God, the world as a ready-made cosmos dies also. Eventually, in the teaching of Nietzsche and his successors we begin to see the emergent conclusion of the whole story when the new fully emancipated type of human being emerges, and we are able to see our own lives, and our world, as our own works of art. There is no real world. Joy in life, joy in creative work, and solar living replace everything that religion has been hitherto. As for 'nihilism', it simply does not worry us: God created *ex nihilo*, and we must now do the same.

If we are indeed currently moving over to a new kind of religious Grand Narrative such as I have described, then it is easy to see how the history of Christianity, its task and its ultimate fate, the accumulating 'Indelible', and 'the West' all fit into the story. The whole Grand Narrative is about the making of humanity; that is, about the emergence at last of fully emancipated and empowered human beings who can bear to look life in the face and say a great 'Yes!' to it. Christianity is the uniquely self-secularizing religious tradition which, with its narratives about the One Creator-God, his incarnation in the man Jesus Christ, his redemptive death, and his gradual self-communication into humanity at large, slowly brings about the formation of the new type of human being. It does this by making a series of indelible impressions upon us. For example:

1 it imprints upon us a new Western kind of selfhood, highly conscious, self-dissatisfied and ready to change;
2 it imprints upon us a new ethic of love: not merely the mutual love of the strong and beautiful for each other, but the ethic of mutual love and forbearance, and compassion for the weak;
3 it teaches us to believe that we can build an orderly, manageable world, in which science and technology are possible;
4 it teaches us to believe in progress: that is, that we can gradually make of ourselves better people in a better world;
5 it teaches us to believe that the full social emancipation of women and of every sort of slave and servant is going to happen;
6 it eventually convinces us that we can live creatively: that is, that we can like artists reimagine and remake ourselves and our world, and that creative joy in life can fully overcome our old fear of nihilism and death.

As Christianity fulfils its historical task by imprinting all this material upon us, it secularizes itself into Western culture – which already increasingly belongs not just to Europe and 'the English-speaking world', but to all human beings everywhere. As this process continues, the old ecclesiastical type of Christianity becomes redundant and disappears, but culturally objectified Christianity goes on and will go on unstoppably until its task is done. Already it is much more fully and generously catholic than 'Catholicism' could ever have hoped to become.

5

Enlightenment Values?

If they did not know it already, people in the West began to understand after the events in Manhattan of 11th September, 2001 that the West is under violent attack by people who detest everything we stand for, and want to destroy us. We gathered also that their hatred is religiously motivated. During the twentieth century everyone had become well adjusted to *ideologically* motivated political enmity, like that of the Nazis for communism, or of the communists for capitalism, but *religiously* motivated hostility as ferocious as this was less familiar. It had been making itself felt ever since the aircraft hijackings and the terrorist attacks on Israel during the 1970s, and then the Islamic revolution of 1979 in Iran that brought down the regime of the Shah and made the country into the Islamic Republic that it still is. So the new vehemently religious anti-Westernism has been around and developing for some 40 years now, but it still perplexes us.

In response, there have been many studies of Wahhabism, of Qutb, and of other neo-puritan people and movements within Islam. The very strength of Islamic conviction is evidently of a kind that we in the West have not ourselves felt since the seventeenth century, reminding us that whereas in the West supernatural faith has been severely weakened or moderated by the application of critical thinking to the Scriptures and the early history of Christianity, Islam has not yet been moderated by the kind of critical study that shows the only-human and culturally relative character of all religious expression. There is Islamic scholarship, but it does not report any conclusions that might seriously disturb the faithful. A few scholars outside the Islamic world have published fully critical-historical works about the Qu'ran and the Hadith, but their conclusions cannot be discussed or even reported within the Islamic world.

What then are we in the West to say and to do in the face of such intense antagonism? They 'hate everything we stand for' – but what *do* we stand for, and how can it be presented in opposition to militant Islam? Although in the West there is Protestant Christian fundamentalism, one cannot really imagine it ever gaining either the numbers or the heart for a 'crusade' against Islam as fierce as the jihad of some Muslims against the West. Not even the strictest American Evangelicals are ever likely to want to play that game. What then do we have to pit against Islamic fundamentalism?

The commonplace answer is: the values of the Enlightenment. They define the essence of the West; they are what Islam hates and we love. They are what, at a pinch, we will all of us agree to fight for. And what is that, you may ask? The one-word answer is usually 'freedom', for when people talk about the values of the Enlightenment they seem to have in mind the ideas that inspired the French and American Revolutions – representative government, government by laws and not by men, freedom under the law, unrestricted freedom of enquiry, expression, public debate, and association, together with freedom of worship and the freedom generally to pursue one's own vision of the good life in one's own way.

It is generally assumed that when you put forward a cluster of ideas such as these, you are describing a secular cultural order that tolerates religion, but is not itself in any way dependent upon religion. People make this assumption because they forget what happened to the doctrine of the Holy Spirit in the sixteenth and seventeenth centuries, and because they have entirely forgotten the old Christian eschatology.

We begin with the Holy Spirit, who was traditionally the

50

third, coequal, consubstantial Person of the divine Trinity. In the Wisdom writings of the Bible the gift of the divine spirit to human beings endows us with our intellectual capacities, especially understanding and wisdom. This idea was revived in the Reformation years when Catholic controversialists said that the Protestant practice of encouraging lay individuals to read the Bible for themselves would lead to doctrinal chaos. To maintain the Church's unity and good order there needs to be an objective teaching authority, vested especially in the papacy, which teaches and enforces the correct interpretation of Scripture. To this Calvin replied that the honest believer reading Scripture has 'the inward testimony of the Holy Spirit' to guide him or her into all truth, as the Lord promised. Everybody has an 'inner light' to guide him: in the seventeenth century it is often called the candle of the Lord, and in the most liberal-minded Puritans – people like the Cambridge Platonists and John Locke – the candle of the Lord becomes just reason. God's Spirit is God's mind, and the indwelling of God's Spirit in every human being is simply everyone's participation in the divine reason. Universal Reason is thus not something self-existent or in any way obvious: it is a secularization of a much older *religious* idea, the idea of the divine Wisdom or Spirit that pervades the cosmos and makes it law-abiding. Reason in us is our own ability to recognize and to follow rules; we are part of creation too, and our reason is a participation in God's reason. Enlightenment rationalism is thus simply a democratization and a laicization of entirely traditional religious themes.

This theological background therefore secures the universality of Enlightenment Reason. There was only one divine Sprit, poured out upon all flesh, and so there is only one Reason for all human beings. Before Hegel, the Enlightenment was not much troubled by the thought that Reason itself might be different in different times and places. There being only one God, there was only one Reason.

Along similar lines it can very easily be demonstrated that

all the other novel, secular and allegedly non-religious new ideas of the Enlightenment are in fact derived directly from the religious tradition. Of course they are. Most Enlightenment thinkers, before the great 'Atheism' controversy that broke over the philosopher J. G. Fichte in 1799, had continued to cling to a minimal version of the old philosophical theism. In Derrida's language, they had dispensed with the personal God of popular religious belief, 'restricted theology', but they clung to the 'general theology' of the philosophers because they needed it to underpin the objectivity of the world and of our knowledge. Thus most Enlightenment thinkers were not yet post-metaphysical. They followed John Locke in holding on to a minimal metaphysics to support their realism, and they remained minimal theists.[28]

The point I make here is neatly illustrated by the American Constitution and the dollar bill ('In God we trust'). The official secularity of the public sphere of life and the clear separation of church and state are combined with – *and actually rest upon!* – an assumed background belief in God that keeps everything stable and objective. You don't need fundamentalism to hold everything in place: just the ghost of the old God will do very nicely, thank you.

There is a similar persistence of ancient religious themes in Enlightenment hopes for the human future. In so far as Enlightenment thinkers hoped for steady historical progress towards a glorious future consummation, they were continuing the old Christian theology of history. Modern people often suppose that religion teaches us to hope for a blessed life after death in heaven, forgetting that the dominant biblical hope was always for the return of Christ and the establishment of the Kingdom of God *upon this earth*. The people of the Enlightenment mostly disliked the power of the visible Church and the way it sought to limit free enquiry and control truth, but the Bible itself assures us that organized religion is only a temporary stopgap, and that in the hoped-for Kingdom-world there will be no organized religion and no class-system. Everyone will be equal

– as indeed they very conspicuously are in the Christian art of Italy and Flanders. Look at any representation of Paradise, and note that everyone looks the same. (Tintoretto's *Paradise* in the Doge's Palace at Venice is an excellent example.) In short, the eschatological hopes of Fourierists, Saint-Simonians, anarchists and socialists were all of them directly derived from the biblical tradition – the only novelty being the conviction that, in the language of Kant, 'the *summum bonum* is immanently realizable'. By social reform we could ourselves bring into being on this earth the better world that humans have always longed for, and we need no longer wait patiently for a special intervention of God to do it all for us.[29] That confidence, that human beings really can better their own lot by their own future actions within the present historical order, is new. But the world that all those communists, anarchists and utopians want to bring into being remains the egalitarian world that *religion* has always taught us to hope for.

So far the appeal to 'the values of the Enlightenment' has not produced anything very much that is essentially and distinctively Western without being also and previously Christian. One important candidate remains, namely what is variously spoken of as critical thinking, free enquiry and 'the independent mind'.

Here we seem to be on firm ground, for surely the church authorities have always and in every age sought in their own interest to control truth and to inhibit freedom of thought and artistic expression? Maybe, but it is worth beginning by recalling Nietzsche's frequent insistence upon the importance of Christian self-examination in pursuit of personal moral and intellectual integrity. The pursuit of an 'examined life' and an integrated selfhood calls for vigilant and scrupulous self-examination; but, says Nietzsche, it was by this route that Christian ethics steadily undermined Christian dogma. If you are to know Truth, your heart must be pure: that is, you must be vigilantly critical and free from any self-deception. To make your whole system strong, you must *purge* it of all errors and inconsistencies. And for Nietzsche – as we have already noted – this was the true beginning of the modern critical type of thinking.[30]

So far as he goes, Nietzsche gets it right; but he does not get it *all* right. Christian self-examination only too easily becomes over-scrupulous to the point of neurotic anxiety. The crucial, brilliant move in early modern times was to shift the focus of scrupulous attention away from one's own self and its motives, and instead to focus it upon the intellectual method that one is using. If the price of liberty is eternal vigilance, the price of truth is continual scrupulosity in examining and refining the rules of evidence and the tests for truth in the area in which you are working. In the long run the public learns to trust the newspaper whose editor sets and demands of his staff the highest journalistic standards, the legal system whose judges are most stringent and objective in their conduct of court proceedings, the scientists whose professional leadership is quickest to expose and punish lapses, and the new pharmaceuticals that have been most rigorously and scrupulously tested. In the long run the unique power and success of modern Western culture owes everything to the rigour and scrupulosity with which the various learned bodies continually set, reappraise, refine and enforce intellectual standards. Critical thinking plays the same sort of role as does the independence of the judiciary in the field of law: while that standard is maintained, all is not lost.

But this makes one aware of how extraordinary is the relation of modern Western culture to the Christian era that preceded it. The modern West is a huge objectification of the old Christian spirituality, transferring to the entire public and intellectual life of the culture the scrupulous spirit of critical examination and purging that the monk in his cell had originally directed against *himself*, and himself alone.

This critical spirit owed something to Socrates, but much more to St Paul and, later, St Augustine. The idea that systematic critical examination and testing is the only way to the Truth we seek began as a principle of Christian spirituality, but its enormous power was discovered only when it was *extraverted*, turned outwards to become a general rule for all fields of enquiry. So the asceticism of the monk was transformed into the professional discipline of the scientist.

How did the extraversion happen? Perhaps its beginning was the criticism by dissenters, from the fourteenth century onwards, of the historical basis for the Western Church's increasingly grandiose claims for itself and for papal authority. This involved historical criticism of the so-called Petrine Commission in St Matthew's Gospel, of the claim that St Peter was the 'first pope', and especially of the so-called Donation of Constantine, a forged document of the early Middle Ages in which the Emperor Constantine purports to give to Pope Sylvester I (AD 314–35) not only dominion over Italy and other Western territories, but also universal primacy over the other Patriarchates in the East. Even before the Reformation, leading Western writers had shown the Donation of Constantine to be a forgery, but the subsequent critique of the Church's claims by Protestant controversialists was more searching, and it laid the foundations for the subsequent development, not only of critical *theology*, but also of critical thinking generally. Thus internal controversies within the Church were the bridge that led Western thought to discover the potential power of critical thinking, when it was extraverted and applied generally to *all* truth-claims, by people like Descartes.

I conclude that the attempt by secularists to give a non-religious account of what Western culture is, and to what it owes its unique values and achievements, is mistaken. Western culture is Christianity objectified and secularized, and it is very close in spirit to liberal Protestantism and the Society of Friends – a thesis that may seem strange to the Eastern Orthodox and Roman Catholic Christians of today, but which will seem platitudinous to historians of the European settlements in the Americas.

6

Progress: The Accumulated Indelible

What is extraordinary about the West is that in it as nowhere else in the world people have escaped the domination of life by tradition. At some time in the past (in fact, surely, in the late seventeenth century) we became confident that we were surpassing the Ancients, the former giants of our culture. We could leave the Old Masters – Plato and Aristotle, the Fathers of the Church – behind us. If we could just get ourselves sufficiently well organized, if we had sufficient bodies of people well trained in the right research techniques, and if we had a political process that allowed criticism, reform and renewal, then we could make indefinite future progress together, and eventually change the human condition permanently for the better.

Ideas about the future secular progress of humanity were both very widely canvassed and very varied during the seventeenth century.[31] They were often linked – as by Francis Bacon himself, the chief pioneer – with claims to have devised a new 'organon' or research method by which new knowledge could be acquired, systematized, vested in a body of people, disseminated and applied. Others emphasized the widening of people's horizons and the increase of wealth that could be brought about by free trade. The politically minded looked to the state to improve the population by eugenic programmes, by legislation and by education, but this prompted fears that if people might be moulded into virtue by the state, then there was perhaps an equal danger that an unscrupulous ruler might use modern knowledge to mould the people for slavery. The thought was sufficient to make many progressive thinkers suspicious of any control of education by the state.

Only gradually did the idea develop that just as in the realm of nature universal laws of motion had been discovered, so also in the 'moral' or human realm there were laws of historical development which guaranteed future progress. Often this strong idea of *inevitable* progress was linked with claims and observations about the steady progress of science (and then, later, of technology). In one form or another traces of this idea linger yet, because after all we do still observe a steady growth of scientific knowledge, rapid technological development, and consequent rapid social change. But it is very noticeable that in modern science-fiction writing and drama there is a bleak and discouraging contrast between the extremely advanced technology on display, and the crude violence of the human beings who operate it. Very few imaginative writers seem able to think in terms of *moral* progress. Not at all; and indeed in the modern German philosophers since Nietzsche the mere increase of knowledge and technical power gives no grounds at all for optimism about human beings and human society as such.[32] On the contrary, technology tends to become the villain of their stories, as our exponentially growing knowledge and power make it possible for us to become violent and barbarous on an ever-larger scale. Since about the 1930s, many or most visions of the long-term human future have been pessimistic.

All these considerations are very familiar, but alongside them runs another doubt. When our thinking has become thoroughly secular, immanent and intra-historical, we see that we can no longer claim to have access to any absolute, extra-human and extra-historical viewpoint or standards. We cannot jump out of time while yet remaining ourselves. In which case, surely words like progress and decline lose meaning, because there is no independent measure of them?

We are always *inside* the historical process, an open-ended stream of conversation and writing within which ideas about morality and values, individual and social, are of course constantly changing. And they are not answerable to anything outside the process, because the process *has* no outside. We, our moral standards, and the moral judgements we make by applying them, are all *within* the historical process. We can of course easily learn something about the moral outlook of another age, but we don't know of any absolute or extra-historical moral outlook.[33]

Darwin himself saw the point in relation to the process of biological evolution. The process itself is not a mind, and it does not value one organism above another. Since Descartes, it has been agreed that nature is a value-free zone. Objectively, the beetle and the blackbird are both of them just products of the process. There is no useful sense in which the blackbird is a 'higher' form of life than the beetle, and no sense in which one of them 'deserves' to survive more than the other. And the point would stand in exactly the same way if we were to write 'human being' and 'scorpion' instead of 'beetle' and 'blackbird'. Of course, any human being can in principle write a history of values which tells the whole story of human ethical and aesthetic valuations in such a way that it culminates in the opinions of himself and others like him in his generation. But then a few decades later someone else may well come along and tell a very different story; and those of their contemporaries who read both stories will not have access to any transcendent and supra-historical standard by which they can tell that one of the two is 'objectively' any wiser than the other.

Thus thoroughgoing historicism combined with a strong belief in progress, is certain eventually to lead to nihilism, as Nietzsche saw with devastating clarity. We have not yet escaped from the position he describes, and I am far from sure that we should even *wish* to escape.

We thus arrive at an interestingly complex puzzle.

First, it may well be said that the West is the culture-area in which people have believed that the future can be better than the past – and what is more, that we can ourselves bring this about by our own efforts. And in fact the West did succeed in making a take-off into sustained and accelerating growth in the late sixteenth century. Since then there has been a blizzard of change, and Western ethics, politics, economics and science-based industrial culture now dominate the globe. And in a broad sense the West still 'believes in progress', for as we look about us it seems to us obvious that too many peoples are kept in a state of needless poverty, backwardness and misery by their own obstinate loyalty to irrational and harmful traditions.

Second, we may ask how far Christianity begat the West's uniquely strong and successful belief in the possibility of progressive 'improvement' (as the eighteenth century called it) or 'development' (the preferred nineteenth-century term). It is true that the dominant Western theology pictured a long history of redemption that moved through a series of half-a-dozen distinct stages, acts or 'dispensations' towards a final glorious consummation of history. But on the orthodox account, surely, the whole drama was entirely controlled by God, and the individual believer could not do more than obediently act out the part scripted for her according to the rules of the particular dispensation in which she found herself?

All that is so, but at the same time there are many indications that human beings may also think of themselves as by their own action doing something to hasten the coming of the future consummation. Adam and Eve were traditionally the first Parents not just of the Jewish people, nor just of the faithful, but of the entire human race, which indicates that the biblical theology of history is – at least by implication – fully global. The Christian Church from early times saw itself as being fully universal, and its history as a story of progressive expansion across the world that had brought it from nowhere to being the established faith of the Roman Empire in less than three centuries. When the whole world was evangelized, the End would come. In fact, church history continued to be written and thought of in terms of steady progress through *human* apostolic work until the early twentieth century. From Eusebius to Latourette the Christian mission was always seen as a *civilizing* mission, and Christianity was therefore seen as a socially progressive force. In which case, surely, the difference between old and new is not very great. In the era dominated by the Church, human progress is brought about by the spread of the gospel, whereas since the Enlightenment human progress is brought about by explorers and merchants, by the critique of Tradition, by the widening of people's horizons and the spread of new ideas, by the steady growth of knowledge, and by the quest in every area of human activity for more efficient organization and production. On which account, perhaps Western culture continues to be a light to the Gentiles, pretty much as the Church has been?

Second, within Christianity there has always been an 'extremist' tradition that attempts to prod God into action and so accelerate the coming of the End, whether it be by voluntary martyrdom, by asceticism, by mysticism, by attempts to establish the Kingdom of Christ on earth by force, or even by extremist radical theology. In some degree Christian faith has always been perceived as being not merely something that commands you to wait patiently until you see it all come true, but also as something that you must *make* true by your own action. Albert Schweitzer of course put Jesus himself in this tradition; and so perhaps did Franz Kafka.[34]

You might expect me then to conclude that on this point, as on others that we have considered, the modern secular idea of progress does not have to be regarded as being atheistic and anti-religious. On the contrary, it has a long prehistory in our religious tradition. But now we have found a complication, which is that, like the closely related idea of thoroughgoing critical thinking, the idea of progress turns out to be incipiently nihilistic. The restless, universally questioning and dissatisfied spirit that drives people in both areas eventually undermines all fixed positions, all supposed 'absolutes' and criteria for evaluation, and even in the end all objectivity. And where there is no longer any agreed and objective unchanging criterion of progress, there is no progress.

We realize this when we recognize that just as in the religious tradition progress is not always smoothly incremental, so *also* in the wider post-Christian cultural tradition the progress of knowledge and the increase of wealth is not smoothly incremental, but involves from time to time major paradigm-shifts and social upheavals, which bring with them great changes in world-view and in morality. Interesting: a biblical change of dispensation, when secularized, becomes a Kuhnian 'paradigm-shift'.

The Bible provides a great illustration. In the Patriarchal Age between Noah and Moses there appears to be no professional priesthood, and any head of a household may perform sacrifices on behalf of his own family. The Patriarchs may take any number of wives and concubines, and may lie to others when it appears to be in their interest to do so. But in the period of the Law that begins with Moses on Sinai there is a professional priesthood, and a very elaborate law-code prescribing the cult at a central Temple, not to mention a good deal of tightening-up in matters of personal morality. Then in the New Testament there is another and very great change of dispensation. The entire 'Ceremonial Law' is abrogated, Gentiles are admitted to the community without circumcision, and the levitical priesthood disappears. The various institutions of a new religion begin to develop.

The Bible hints at other dispensations, and in particular we are told of a Paradisal Age at the very beginning, while at the end, after the age of the Church has been ended by the return of Christ, there will be a Millennium, or 'Kingdom' period of a thousand years during which Christ and his saints will rule over a renewed world. There are thus at least five major dispensations within the biblical salvation-history, and we gather that the changeover from each dispensation to the next may involve very great changes in world-view, in theology, in institutions, in religious life and in morality. It seems therefore that religious and moral truth are *not* absolute, but are relative to the particular dispensation under which we take ourselves to be living.

There may be disagreement about which dispensation we now live under. The Jewish people are still around, and they of course consider themselves to be still living in the age of the Mosaic Law. Ecclesiastical Christians take themselves to be living in the years of grace, during which it is the prime duty of the Church to get the gospel preached worldwide; and there are also some Kingdom-Christians, who consider that the ecclesiastical period, in which the (priestly) hierarchy rule the Church, control the sacraments and so on, is already long over. Of these Kingdom-Christians the most important remaining group are the Friends, or 'Quakers'. In their view the changeover from the Age of the Church to the Kingdom period is the religious face of the parallel changeover from absolute monarchy to liberal democracy in Western politics. And indeed in their organization and their ethical witness the Friends are very strongly modern and liberal-democratic in temper.

Now the interesting question arises: Does the Bible help us to decide under which of these three dispensations we are now living? No: it does not, although if your copy of the Bible happens to be in English and to have the New Testament printed at the end, I think we may presume that you suppose yourself to be living in either the ecclesiastical period or the Kingdom period.

There is also a further complication. A very large number of people assert that the Biblical salvation-history has been considerably revised by the appearance of a last Prophet and the giving of a final revelation from God, in the year AD 622 by the old reckoning. This last Prophet has inaugurated a new age on earth, dated from the year of his migration (*hijra*) with his earliest followers from Mecca to Medina. In this age the people of God (the *umma*) practise Islam and live under Islamic law, until 'the Day', the Day of Judgement, which marks the beginning of the next and final dispensation.

We now have at least six dispensations, and four possible views about the dispensation under which we are now living. They are the views held respectively by the Jews, by ecclesiastical Christians, by the Friends and by Muslims, and it is not at all easy – as G. E. Lessing and many others have pointed out – to find terms on which the various parties can discuss and negotiate their differences. Indeed, the parties are usually found to have little appetite for any such discussions.

The question arises: Why do not the various believers themselves notice how deeply and subtly the implied historical-cultural relativity of all matters of faith and morals pervades *their own* traditions? The answer is, presumably, that the mass of ordinary believers accept dogmatically the teachings and the outlook of their own dispensation, as it is understood in their own day – and otherwise, they leave it at that. They do not wish to think about the relation of religious truth to history.

For scholars who study the history of religions, however, some sort of historical-cultural relativism is clearly unavoidable. Nothing is absolute, partly because we learn that our version of religious truth has a beginning in time, and also because during the long historical development of the tradition it seems that *all* ideas, institutions, values and interpretations are open to change. For history as for critical thinking, and for religious thought as for scientific thought, nothing is sacrosanct and everything is in principle negotiable. The only unchanging truth is the truth of universal 'impermanence'. Everything flows, and nothing is anchored.

I hope I have said enough now to prepare you for a bolder statement. If the genius of Buddhism (in the Middle Way tradition that stems from Nagarjuna) is to have made great religion out of nihilism, then we can reply that Christianity evidently itself also includes a nihilistic moment – a 'speculative Good Friday' – within its movement of self-understanding. There has to be that time of pure death and darkness, and you have to become familiar with it if you are to understand the Christian tradition.

Very well. Now, more largely, the genius of the West as a cultural system generally *also* lies in its nihilism. The West is a cultural tradition based upon a spirit of passionate, perpetual, restless criticism, self-criticism and doubt that keeps it perpetually reforming itself, innovating and reinventing. The West is nihilistic, in the sense that for it nothing is fixed except the principle that nothing is fixed. The West is based upon the Death of God; that is, upon a constant attempt to establish a great principle of supreme reality, intelligibility and value, and upon the repeated *failure* of that attempt. Over and over, we build, and what we build collapses. We posit God, and God dies.

The dialectic I am referring to here forever oscillates between dogmatism and scepticism, between affirmation and negation. It begins even in pre-Christian times, when the Greek philosophical schools – and especially Plato's Academy – swung back and forth between dogmatism and scepticism, but the culminating illustration of it is the central Christian symbol of the Godman dead upon the cross.

Now an even higher peak blocks our way: it is the question of Sisyphus. I have been saying that the genius of the West lies in its endless and seemingly insatiable self-questioning and discontent. It constantly struggles to establish a satisfactory world-view and moral order, but as soon as it seems to have succeeded, it must begin to undermine itself again. The West is indeed something wonderful. It is, by some distance, the most interesting and powerful cultural tradition that has yet appeared upon the human scene. But it cannot help but know by now that the endless questioning and innovation that makes it so creative also ensures that it can never 'get anywhere' – as people say: I mean that it can never attain the objective reality, truth and value that it is condemned for ever to seek. Is not the West then a futile project?[35] What can keep us going, if we already know that we cannot win?

The answer to this puzzle is that although it is true that the whole historical process is immanent and outsideless, and that therefore we can have no truly independent criterion of progress, *within* the process there can occur small indelible or irreversible advances in understanding, and the accumulation of these is a sort of progress that we *can* still believe in.

In general, I accept postmodern nihilism. There is indeed nothing but the beginningless, endless and outsideless conversation of humanity; and we have no way of moving to some external standpoint outside the conversation, from which we might be in a position to judge that some bits of it are better, or nearer the Truth, than others. There is only the cultural flux, within which (as people say) 'the pendulum swings' endlessly back and forth. But within the conversation small things may happen that change us irreversibly or indelibly, and we earlier suggested that one way of looking at a religious tradition and appraising it is to ask ourselves: 'In what ways has this tradition affected us indelibly; what seemingly permanent differences has it made to us?'

There are secular examples of such indelible change. There is, for example, the change from innocence to experience, a change from which there is no return. In social ethics, one might similarly claim that the change from tribalism to nationalism, and then from nationalism to internationalism is (or should be) irreversible. It involves a widening of one's horizons, a broadening of one's sympathies, that one cannot rationally regret or give up.

As well as these non-religious examples, I have suggested a number of small indelible differences that Christianity has already made to us all, differences that we cannot give up. As listed in Chapter 4 above, they were:

1 Christianity's picture of the human being as chronically highly conscious and self-dissatisfied.
2 Various ethical principles including
   a the ethic of mutual love and forbearance;
   b the principle that no human being should be treated as simply expendable, because each human being is in principle unique and redeemable; and
   c the orientation of the ethic of love especially *not* towards the strong and the beautiful, but towards the weakest and most vulnerable.
3 The principle of the uniformity of nature, interpreted simply as claiming that we can expect to be capable of building a coherent world-picture, and effective technologies.
4 The belief that although there is no objective purposiveness out there at all, we can hope to be able to make some real progress by gradually accumulating a series of small, indelible gains such as these.

Of these four indelibles, (1) is derived historically from the old Christian doctrine of man and ultimately from St Paul; (2) is derived from Christian ethics; (3) is derived from the old doctrine of creation; and (4) is derived for the old Christian idea of the working-out of our redemption within history. A fifth indelible (5), the belief that human beings can be creative, is based precisely upon our coming to see our whole religious history as a progressive transfer of power from God to human beings.

Interestingly, on my account Christianity continues to work, and goes on making small indelible differences to us, long after we have ceased to believe in any of the old supernatural dogma, and long after we have abandoned the Church. Nobody in the West can be wholly non-Christian. We cannot help continuing to be influenced by the old dreams, as for example Marxists, anarchists, utopians,

Martin Luther King, John Lennon and Jürgen Habermas were when they all continued to pursue some version of the old biblical vision of a fully reconciled, free and open future society, the messianic Kingdom here on this earth. Whether or not you personally think of yourself as being a Christian does not very much affect the extent to which Christianity goes on influencing your hopes and your dreams. Hence the curious fact that although the modern EU seems to have largely repudiated its Christian past, it nevertheless continues to be deeply influenced by it. You may call yourself a non-Christian, but the dreams you dream are still Christian dreams, and you continue to be part of the history of Christianity. That's your fate. You may consider yourself secular, but the modern Western secular world is *itself* a Christian creation.

7

The West as Modernity

People who hate the West so much that they are willing to sacrifice their own lives in the struggle against it often seem to do so because they see the West as Modernity itself, an almost-irresistible future that threatens to overwhelm them and destroy everything they hold dear. The West is the Great Satan, or even the Scarlet Woman who to Third-World puritans is both intensely seductive and intensely repellent at once. The very fact that she is so alluring to them convinces them that they must convert her effect upon them into the will to destroy her.

How did this extremely violent love–hate relationship with the West develop? In classical antiquity the most obvious reference of the East–West contrast was to the Mediterranean world. The Bishop of Rome was the Patriarch of the West, and his jurisdiction extended over what we would now call Italy, France, Spain, Britain and the Western provinces of North Africa. But Rome in late Antiquity was very far from being the centre of the world. On the contrary, the bulk of the Empire's population and wealth, and three of the four Christian Patriarchs, were in the East. Then in AD 330 Constantine established the new imperial city at Constantinople. The city soon became the New Rome, and its bishop a fifth Patriarch. In due course, he even became the Oecumenical Patriarch of the East, and a serious rival to the Bishop of Rome.

Against this background it is easy to understand that the West seemed to many to be out on a limb, together the edge of the known world and relatively marginal – even backward.[36] And for centuries after the fall of the city, Rome was indeed rather ruinous and backward. It could afford only very modest architecture compared with the splendour of Byzantium, and its Patriarch was venerated but impov- erished. Yet the Lord had promised to be with his apostles on their journeys to the ends of the earth, and St Paul him- self, according to Clement, had travelled to 'the limit of the Occident'[37] – that is, even to Spain. The Pillars of Hercules at Gibraltar were one of the four corners of the earth, the furthest point West. Beyond them lay, perhaps, mythical places like Atlantis. Then as now, the West was legendary and attractive, but relatively unpeopled as compared with the rich and densely populated East.

Even after the Eastern Christian Empire fell and was re- placed by the Empire of the Ottoman Turks, the old weight- ing towards the East persisted, a weighting which still appears in Wordsworth's opening lines about Venice:

Once she did hold the gorgeous East in fee,
And was the safeguard of the West ...[38]

Even in early modern times, Western Christian Europe still felt obliged to acknowledge the superiority of Islam and 'the gorgeous East'. But as a sea power and as a trading port Venice, together with a few other ports – Barcelona, Genoa – was powerful enough in the Western and Central Mediter- ranean to keep the might of Islam at bay; and Venice took care to maintain coolly friendly relations with Istanbul.

This history helps to explain why the consciousness of something called 'Western Civilization' (seen of course as centring in France and neighbouring lands of Western Europe) developed only so very late. During the first millen- nium Western Christian Europe seemed relatively inferior to the East, and then in later times, when the Eastern Church was largely in a state of political subjection, the lands of the Christian West could not easily claim to equal the splen- dour of the Arab *calif* and the Turkish Sultan. The West's strength grew only gradually as its explorers and merchants, followed by colonial planters and settlers and then by engineers building railways, gradually swarmed over the whole world. Britain, France, Spain, Portugal and other countries developed very large overseas empires – and now, in the second half of the nineteenth century, we at last begin to hear talk of something called 'Western Civilization' which has a newly constructed but lengthy pedigree and a unique mission to the rest of humanity.[39]

This helps to explain why the West, in so many eyes, just *is* modernity. In Japan, for example, there had been intermittent and only moderately successful Christian missionary efforts for three centuries, before in 1859 'the West' suddenly arrived in force, and the modern world hit Japan and changed it irreversibly. 'The West' meant political power, trade, science-based industry, modern communications, and a hurricane of new ideas.

Yet the West remains symbolically ambivalent. Japan, out in the 'Orient', was and still is the land of the rising sun, whereas the West was always the 'Occident', the land of the declining sun and of the dead. In ancient Egypt they built the cities of the living on the east bank of the Nile, and of the dead on the west bank. A loose symbolic association between sunset and death persists to this day:

Let me be gathered to the quiet West,
The sundown splendid and serene,
Death.[40]

The association is easy, and almost too easily moving:

Comrade, look not on the West;
'Twill have the heart out of your breast.[41]

But during the same early modern period in Europe another meaning of the West was preparing. Explorers who sailed between the Pillars of Hercules at the western edge of the world passed over the ocean of Atlantis, hoping to find a mythic land of fabulous wealth, a New World, a Far West beyond the old West. What they found and the language they used in speaking of it still reflects something of that glamour and that heightened expectation. A New-Found Land, indeed a whole new western hemisphere in which colonists might hope to build a new society. The Irish philosopher George Berkeley, writing in about 1729, at a time when he was hoping to attract funding for a new college in what we now call Bermuda, evokes and extends the old-Western philosophy of history:

> Westward the course of empire takes its way;
>   The first four acts already past,
> The fifth shall close the drama with the day:
>   Time's noblest offspring is the last.[42]

The 'four acts' seem ambiguous. Berkeley might intend us to read him politically: the great centre of civilization has shifted westwards from Mesopotamia to Egypt, to Greece and then to Rome. Now it takes its greatest leap, across the Atlantic to America. But in the background there is surely an echo of biblical dispensationalism: the four acts are the ages of Paradise, the Patriarchs, the Mosaic Law and the Church. Now in the New World refugees from the persecuting churches of Europe will build in America the long-awaited Kingdom of God on earth.

Could Berkeley, who was very much a churchman, have entertained such ideas? Perhaps he could: we tend to forget that Christianity is nowadays a largely forgotten religion. People have forgotten that the ecclesiastical phase of Christianity, which is so decayed, was only ever meant to be a temporary expedient and a second-best. They simply equate ecclesiastical Christianity and its very far-fetched doctrine system with the real thing, Christianity itself, fully realized. But the Church is not Christianity, and never can be. It is merely a systematic deferral of Christianity, a kind of Berlin

Wall that has been in place for too long and now needs to come down. The Church is like Ellis Island, one of those immigrants' reception centres where people are kept waiting, under discipline and semi-imprisoned, until the day when they are released into full membership of the larger society that they long to become part of. In the eighteenth century people still understood that when they said in the Lord's Prayer, 'Thy Kingdom come', they really *meant* it. Even Kant, Hegel and Schleiermacher still knew that Church-Christianity was scheduled to pass over into the Kingdom-religion that will succeed it. All three of them saw humanity as now becoming adult, and at long last outgrowing the repressive boarding-school culture of the Church. They saw the transition as taking place in their own age.

At the time of the Reformation, many Europeans thought in these terms. They migrated to America in the hope that there they might throw off the old structures of religious and political domination. They hoped that in America the Kingdom of God might be built on earth. People would no longer need other-worldly illusions, and they would not need to be ruled either by monarchs or by priests, if only they could build a society in which the common life of the common people was completely free and satisfactory to them. Just classless, vernacular speech and living would have epic simplicity and dignity. People would be content with ordinariness.

This equation of 'the West' with America and with a new life in the New World became and remained very potent for a long time. In the largest English industrial towns there were until quite recently Mormon offices that gave advice and help to people who were thinking of emigrating in order to join the dream. 'Go West, young man, and grow up with the country!' was a famous piece of advice.[43] As the USA became politically and economically unified by such achievements as the completion of the railroad through the mountains to Sacramento, writers like Walt Whitman articulated the country's growing sense of its own enormous potential.

Against this background the USA became in the twentieth century not only the leading country of the West, but more, the country that personifies 'the West-as-modernity-itself'; a country weighed down by perhaps too much messianic consciousness of itself, too many hopes and dreams, too much symbolism. How could it possibly fulfil such vast expectations? But even today the hopes and dreams are still alive: among the Arabs the USA is still reportedly the country that is both the most loved *and* the most hated of all lands on earth.

Ironically, it is in precisely the areas where the USA professes to be the most secular and the most rational of countries that one is most aware of the power of old religious dreams. Church and state are officially quite distinct, and public life is secular and supposedly based on Enlightenment rationality. But at the same time the state is also the Day of Pentecost enacted: human beings from every nation gathered and become one new nation, *E pluribus unum*. Everything in America's public life reeks of Christianity, and a version of Christianity that is much more up-to-date, rational and interesting than the version of Christianity that is purveyed by the popular preachers.[44] Perhaps it is because the Arabs from their own related but extra-Christian point of view see all this so clearly that they react to it all so ambivalently.

So if 'the West' is modernity itself, and nowadays is above all America, then the EU is wrong. The West is still Christian; but it is not the Christianity of the Church that counts nowadays, but the new West's post-ecclesiastical Christian *culture*. Read Walt Whitman's *Leaves of Grass* and the prose collection *Democratic Vistas* for a taste of it.

Many people in Europe will have none of all this. They don't accept the basic premiss, to the effect that the church version of Christianity is now historically obsolete and that we should all of us have moved over to the Kingdom version at least two hundred years ago. Then, in addition, the European objectors will add that the original American dream has long ago been completely overlaid, corrupted and lost. Too much nationalist messianism, too much love of money, wealth and power, and too little appreciation of the extent to which in the media age capitalism corrupts the whole culture – all this has so swamped the original ideals that they have now become unrealizable. Take a look, they will say, at Jean Baudrillard's portrait of America.[45]

Few people will claim that *America* is one of Baudrillard's very best works. Too often he merely describes the visual impressions of a detached, floating observer, and the effect is rather as if someone had written an essay about the social and cultural life of modern Japan on the basis of nothing more than Tokyo street scenes at night, crowded with those huge blaring illuminated signs that can mean nothing to Westerners who don't know the language. But Baudrillard also has a passage that is close to our present interests, in his section 'Utopia achieved'. His argument is that the new revolutionary social and philosophical thinking released in Europe by the French Revolution never crossed the Atlantic. Perhaps he means that the War of Independence was only an anti-colonial war: it did not have the same profound cultural consequences as the European revolutions were to have.

> ... the Americans kept intact ... the utopian and moral perspective of the men of the eighteenth century, or even of the Puritan sects of the seventeenth, transplanted and kept alive, safely sheltered from the vicissitudes of history ... From the beginning the sects played the major role in the movement towards an achieved utopia ... they it is who strive to bring about the Kingdom of God on Earth, whereas the Church restricts itself to the hope of salvation and (the) theological virtues.
>
> It is as though America as a whole had embraced this sect-like destiny: the immediate concretization of all perspectives of salvation.[46]

In effect, Baudrillard is saying that whereas in Europe people's hopes for a better world came to be expressed in the form of political demands for a revolutionary transformation of society and all its institutions, in America it is as if the whole country wants to follow the sect's way to salvation: utopia now, instant conversion and beatification, moral transformation, an improvement in one's material fortunes, a solid assurance of one's own righteousness. And all this, based upon intense self-criticism and belief in the possibility of repentance and a change of heart; for indeed nobody could accuse Americans of not being self-critical.

Baudrillard's *America* is 20 years old now, and its assumption that America continues to be the old white, Anglo-Saxon, Protestant America is dated in these days when Mexican and other Latino immigration is rapidly bringing Catholic and Protestant numbers into parity. But his remarks about the continuing influence upon the whole culture of the values of the small Protestant sect are very striking. Consider recent American cinema in such genres as the thriller, the police procedural, science-fiction, the western and so on: to an extraordinary degree the most important single motif driving such films is the almost *cosmic* importance of the lone individual's battle to preserve himself and his moral integrity, and to gain public vindication in the face of the sinister forces that threaten him. If in a sense America *is* modernity, then the old Protestant Christian – and indeed, sectarian – values are still surprisingly important and prominent, even when on the surface the film seems to be entirely secular, and to contain no overtly religious language.

8

Modernity as a State of Exile

Religious ideas are astonishingly tenacious, and we can be relied upon to put them through any number of transformations before we abandon them altogether. Perhaps the best example of this is the interpretation of human life in historical time as a journey. For around three millennia it has been very widely felt that our life is lived in something like a state of exile. We are not where we should be: some primal sin or disaster has caused us to be banished from our true home, of which we have dim, golden memories. We have been sent out into the world of historical time, and there we are condemned to undertake a very long march, borne up (if we are lucky) by a far-off hope of final redemption.

The finest expression in our literature of this interpretation of human existence occurs at the end of *Paradise Lost*. The primal couple, Adam and Eve, must leave Paradise and go out together into the uncertainties of history:

> They, looking back, all the eastern side beheld
> Of Paradise, so late their happy seat,
> Waved over by that flaming brand; the gate
> With dreadful faces throng'd, and fiery arms.
> Some natural tears they dropt, but wiped them soon;
> The world was all before them, where to choose
> Their place of rest, and Providence their guide:
> They, hand in hand, with wandering steps and slow,
> Through Eden took their solitary way.[47]

The lost world of Paradise was a temporal world, but its time was not linear, historical time. It was the original,

76

mythic sort of time that English speakers invoke when they use phrases such as 'in those days we always used to ... (do so-and-so)', or the time that is referred to when we begin a story for children with the phrase 'Once upon a time ...'. What had happened to Adam and Eve was that awareness of their freedom had led to the consciousness of sin, and so to their expulsion out of Eden and into historical time.

Their life changes utterly. In Eden everything was familiar, and every day was the same. Now they are plunged into a radically uncertain, contingent world in which, as people say, 'You never know what tomorrow may bring.' But happily they are not just passive victims of circumstance, drifting and constantly buffeted. Their own form of consciousness, the sense of sin, preserves for them a faint, indirect memory of the world they have lost, and tells them that they do remain morally free. They still have some ability, by choosing this and rejecting that, to shape their own future course. And towards what else can they steer themselves except some kind of recovery – perhaps in a different form – of the blessed world that they have lost? So they do have something to hope for, and they may see in the very fact that they have been able to reach this understanding of their new condition an indication that they are not quite alone. They do have Providence for their guide: something *destines* them.

In this account we notice very striking links between the openness and uncertainty of historical existence and our human self-consciousness, as the *consciousness* of being one who is a *sinner*, and *exiled*, but yet still *free*, and a pilgrim with a future *hope*.[48] Such is, or was, the classical Western Christian analysis of the condition of historical human beings like ourselves. Milton's noble yet downbeat lines manage to suggest it all, so that his epic leaves us looking towards a sequel.

A consequence of this account is the further doctrine that human history was not part of the Creator's original design. History is secondary; it has been created only in response to the Fall of Man. It is the stage on which God plans to direct the long drama of human redemption. History is for sinners; it is the landscape through which they wander on their long journey towards their final salvation. They have – you may say – a debt to pay off and a glorious reward to win, for now we see in this classic understanding of human life the background to the Protestant work ethic. Again quoting popular Anglo-Saxon phrases, we humans need to be 'doing something to justify our own existence': 'We've got something to prove.' Hence the common suggestion that the Western Christian doctrine of man, deeply impressed upon a whole cultural tradition and perhaps especially upon everyone influenced by Calvinism, created the driving energy out of which has come modern Western science-based, capitalist industrial civilization, by far the most powerful and creative human cultural order yet to appear among human beings. Within one lifetime, in the USA, you might have witnessed the entire development from Orville and Wilbur Wright's first powered flight in 1903 to the moon landings of 1968. Can it really be the case that such prodigious achievement was ultimately powered by the religious thought transmitted to us in a slim line of texts – Genesis, Romans, Augustine, Calvin, John Bunyan? Is the culture of the modern West, which fills the whole of humanity with such intense admiration, envy and hatred, simply the last child of Western theology?

The answer is 'Yes': the Western Christian doctrine of man has been that potent. I suggested earlier that modern Western culture is traditional Christian culture extraverted; that is, turned outwards and objectified socially. Christianity is the self-outing and self-secularizing religion that objectifies its own spirituality. Thus the believer's scrupulous self-examination of his own soul, when extraverted, becomes the rigorous and systematic practice of critical thinking and testing that has created modern knowledge; and the believer's consciousness of sin and his consequent effort to work out his salvation by moral striving, when extraverted, becomes the Protestant work ethic which was so fabulously energetic that it could colonize a wilderness and build a developed country such as Australia in only two or three lifetimes.[49]

There is a further point, made well if a little obscurely by Baudrillard when he said (as we saw earlier) that modern American society has preserved much of the sect-like culture in which it began.[50] In the feverish intensity of the sect, the whole gamut of religious feeling and experience is made present and intensely real to the believer: the conviction of sin, the striving to win God's favour, repentance and conversion, and the believer's anticipatory enjoyment of eternal happiness. In the sect, you can 'have it all', at once, and *now*. This Baudrillard refers to as 'the immediate concretization of all perspectives of salvation'. Extraverted, it creates a culture in which the very same people devote themselves furiously, in the same day, to energetic guilt-driven *production* during their working hours and then to equally energetic hedonistic *consumption* during their leisure hours. It is very striking that contemporary English people show how vividly aware they are of the complementarity and the rivalry of these two sides of our life by using the popular phrase, '*the work/life balance*'. 'Work' is paid, productive labour, and 'life' is consumption, enjoyment, so that 'getting your work/life balance right' means 'not working such long, hard hours that you are too tired to enjoy life'.

I don't wish to become involved here in discussing the merits of these ideas, but only to return at this point to Baudrillard. In the small Protestant sect, with its very intense life, the different aspects or stages of the spiritual life tend to become telescoped: self-examination, the conviction of sin, repentance, conversion, the living of a new life, fellowship with the Lord, joy in salvation – everything seems to happen all at once, much as the Puritan preacher used to work his way through the entire Plan of Salvation in every single sermon. Modern secular life is like that. Work and play, tragedy and frivolity, boredom and panic – violent contrasts of mood are part of the daily media bombardment and part of urban life, as if we are all nowadays like the parish priest who must go straight from a wedding breakfast to a death-bed. The Church, with its daily and yearly rounds of worship, pictures eternal salvation as being at the end of a very long and highly routinized journey through life, and death, and purgatory; whereas the popular revivalist preachers of today offer instant conversion and blessedness to an age in which ordinary people have been led to expect that they can indeed have instant everything. Both the sect and modern consumerism promise us that we can *have it all*, right now.

We have been thinking about the huge, and still continuing influence of the old Western Christian picture of the human condition: human beings as pilgrims through historical time, highly conscious, aware of being in a condition of exile from a lost paradisal world and conscious of themselves therefore as sinners, but also as free, as guided by divine providence in their daily moral struggles, and buoyed up by the hope of final salvation – presumably on the far side of death, but with a real foretaste now. It is a very rich and complex picture, and it is not surprising that there are still so many echoes of it in our own contemporary language and experience. In addition, we have remarked on the influence of the small Protestant sect, influenced by Calvinism, in whose intense life all the various stages of the long history of salvation-history tend to become telescoped together in the present moment.

Now, to add to the complications, until the Enlightenment it was generally believed that there really had been a primal couple specially created by God, and living in a state of original righteousness. But with the rise of modern secular knowledge that notion had to be abandoned.[51] This meant that the powerful old myth of Paradise and the Expulsion from Eden must henceforth be interpreted allegorically. But how? We feel that we are not what we should be, and perhaps not what we once were. We are exiles from a lost golden age, who find ourselves condemned to wander through history like Cain. What have we lost?

There are three main psychological interpretations. The transition from Eden to history may be compared with:

1a birth, when we were separated from our original blessedness in the womb and thrust painfully out into individual existence;

1b the end of childhood, when we left the relatively timeless, peaceful and protected world of the child on reaching the age of reason and adolescence, and we began to experience permanent personal turmoil;

1c the need to leave the peaceful daily routines of domestic life, which is relatively extra-historical, and go out into the cold competitive public world to make a living.

There are at least four main social interpretations. The transition from Eden to historical life may be compared with the transitions:

2a from savagery to civilization;

2b from rural, agricultural life to urban, industrial life;

2c from the monastery, which is designed to be sheltered and extra-historical, out into 'the world';

2d from medieval life in the ages of faith dominated by the Church, the liturgical year and a more-or-less cyclical experience of time, to the early modern period when people deliberately stepped out of the sacred world, losing the old 'eternal return of the same' and the old certainties, and chose instead the uncertainties of history.

What is the lost idyll on each of these four accounts? It is the tribe, it is the old rural way of life bound to the land and the seasons, it is the routine of life in a house of religion, and finally, it is the religion-based civilization of the Middle Ages. In each case, we begin from the observations that although modern life is so long and prosperous and secure, we are not as happy as might be expected. We feel blighted, or exiled. So we try to tell a story about the Golden Age from which we have been exiled, we try to identify the moment when things went wrong and we '*lost it*' (as the saying goes), and then we begin to construct a story about how we have since come to the place where we now are and how we may one day come full circle and recover the lost world – perhaps at a higher level.

In effect, the human search for 'meaning' still very often leads us to tell a great story of fall and redemption. There are many familiar political versions of such stories, and they have played a prominent part in the history of ideas. Not least, in modern Germany.

9

Stories about Modernity

The adjective 'modern', from Latin *modo*, 'just now', means 'of or relating to the present time'. In the Western Christian tradition its first use was in the phrase *devotio moderna*, the new style of individual piety that from the late fourteenth century spread, through informal associations of clerics and laypeople, from the Low Countries and down the Rhine to parts of France, Germany and Italy. The *devotio moderna* was new in being relatively more urban, informal, lay and Christ-centred than had been usual in the past. Its best-known writer, Thomas à Kempis, was a contemporary of painters like Jan van Eyck and Roger van der Weyden, which indicates that the period was indeed one in which the focus of religious interest was beginning to switch towards the individual human being and this world.

The greatest figure this tradition produced was Desiderius Erasmus (1466–1536), who after 1500 emerged as perhaps Western Europe's first celebrity intellectual. Still a Catholic, he was also a modern man who owed his huge popularity to his modern 'voice', his markedly independent personal style. His air of being a mocking, free individual certainly sold his books, but eventually it turned both Catholic and Protestant leaders against him. He quarrelled with Luther, who called him a sceptic, and after his death Rome banned his writings.

In later times men like Erasmus – people such as his English friends John Colet and Thomas More – came to be seen as standing on the boundary between two worlds, the medieval and the modern. Defining these two worlds, and explaining why and how the former of them declined and gave way to the latter is not easy.

Certainly one should not at this point resort to the long-popular metaphors which imply that, like individuals, civilizations and cultural epochs eventually grow old and tired. So why *did* the Middle Ages have to end? The art and architecture of the fifteenth century, and then up to the Lutheran revolt, remain splendidly vigorous and humanistic. They do not *look* as if they are in decline. Recent archaeological and historical work on the great monasteries indicates that many of them were economically well-run and prosperous businesses, and technologically surprisingly advanced for their date – especially in metallurgy. So much so, indeed, that one begins to suspect that, even if there had been no Reformation, the monasteries might themselves have been able to contribute to the scientific and the industrial revolutions. Imagine the great religious orders as modern multinational corporations!

In the history of ideas, the standard account of the end of the Middle Ages points to problems in Christian philosophy. From the fourteenth century the old Augustinian synthesis of Christian 'wisdom' declined, and thought moved towards an extreme voluntarism of God's absolute, inscrutable Will. Very pessimistic, this doctrine implies that nothing can be fully explained and understood by humans. The result was nominalism, scepticism, and a break-up of the great synthesis at just the point when it was most needed if a rapidly expanding culture was to be contained successfully.

The difficulty with this story is that it follows Hegel in wanting to see the history of philosophy as being somehow the core of all history. But this is implausible. Before printing, exactly how many people ever read the very few available manuscripts of people like William of Ockham or Gabriel Biel? And were that handful of people in a position to determine the subsequent development of the culture? It sounds unlikely. In the Galileo case we can surely say confidently that by condemning Galileo the Church inflicted a mortal wound upon itself, because we can be quite sure that the host of people who *had* read Galileo's published writings included some who were in a position to determine the subsequent development of the culture. They were the people we would now call the scientists, people who recognized at once that Galileo was right and the Roman authorities were wrong. They knew or guessed that control over cosmology was slipping out of the hands of the priests and being seized by the exponents of the new natural philosophy. The Church was losing power over the commanding heights of the culture. The future must belong to those who sided with Galileo, and continued in his line of work. Beyond a doubt, that was obvious at the time – at least, to the people who mattered – and this was indeed a case where an episode in the history of ideas was of fundamental importance for history generally. But it seems very unlikely that anyone can similarly demonstrate just how the course of late-medieval philosophy brought about the end of the Middle Ages.

What, then, did? Overseas exploration and trade, the rise of a powerful new class of merchants and other assertive townspeople, printing, vernacular languages, lay culture and, soon, an explosion of new knowledge. And we are not talking about various well-known high middle-class households: we are also talking about secular politics and the nation-state. The Church never really tried to be totalitarian: it had always left a space for secular politics and lay culture generally. Now that secular sphere began to expand uncontrollably, and inevitably it soon broke out beyond the bounds of church orthodoxy. Since the Church could not itself teach people how to live richer secular lives, they looked for instruction to the classical authors and artists of ancient Greece and Rome.

And the new 'modern' culture? It took time to find its feet, of course. In Shakespeare's theatre secular politics and social life and even secular private life are still being invented. But what *does* go back to the beginning of modernity is what we noted in Erasmus: the independent, critical

mind, self-aware, ironical, restlessly curious and dissatisfied, and always insisting upon looking at everything, not
from the point of view of objective Authority, but from its
own individual human viewpoint.

In this connection, some commentators use the term
anthropocentrism, as if we were talking about a shift away
from the objective rationalism of medieval thought towards
a naively, innocently human-centred way of thinking; and
other commentators (such as Hans Blumenberg) speak of
human *self-assertion*, as if what we are talking about here
were a presumptuous human rebellion against divine authority. Both of these groups will wish to go on to tell a Fall-story
about how at the end of the Middle Ages the great objective
disciplinary Order of Reason cracked. 'Man' began to put
his own subjectivity first, as if he didn't even wish to hear
about anything but his own hunches and his own point of
view; or alternatively 'Man' rebelled violently against God
and usurped the throne of God, putting himself in the place
of God. In these stories, modernity is seen as arising from
a lazy human forgetting of God, or as a presumptuous but
successful human revolt against God.

Such polemics are, however, unfair to Erasmus. He is not
being naively self-centred, nor is he trying to organize a political revolt against God. It is rather that he simply cannot
be silenced by traditional demands that he defer to Authority and accept various beliefs dogmatically. He cannot help
needing to check everything out for himself. I want to be
sure, he says, and I cannot feel satisfied until I have tested
it all out on my own pulse – meaning, I have to check it out
against my own heart, my own feeling for life. And, no, I
do not have to be described as a sceptic, for you may just as
well see me as standing in the tradition of Jewish *chutzpah*,
which goes on unstoppably questioning and bargaining
even in the presence of God himself. Even Jesus is reported
– when under extreme pressure – as questioning and doubt-
ing God, for that obdurately, irrepressibly questioning spirit
is itself also part of the central Christian tradition.

These observations lead us now to the two principal stories about what modernity is, and how it originated. Modern German history has produced some of the most extreme, and indeed terrifying, illustrations of what modernity may perhaps be and where it may be leading us, and it is not surprising that at the end of the 1940s people should have begun telling stories in answer to the question 'Where did it all go wrong?' Karl Löwith, in *Meaning in History* (1949), argued that a number of the leading ideas of modernity, and in particular the idea of progress, were no more than secularizations of traditional Christian ideas.[52] As such, in Löwith's view, these ideas were 'illegitimate' – meaning, it seems, that they were not as fresh and independent as their proponents claimed, but were mere bastardizations of Christian ideas that properly belonged in a very different context.

To this, Blumenberg replied with *Die Legitimität der Neuzeit* (1966), which tells a very different story.[53] At the end of the Middle Ages Christian culture ran into severe difficulties. God seemed to be becoming more remote,[54] the old theistic metaphysics was being undermined by scepticism, and the whole relation of the human being to the world was threatened. In this time of crisis, modernity arose as the result of a purely human effort to rethink everything. The new starting point was human experience, or (as we have already remarked) one's own pulse, or one's own feeling for life. But as part of its apologetics it needed to have ready to hand some prepared answers to the old stock questions and something to put in the place of the various old certainties. In Blumenberg's language, it needed to 're-occupy' various old positions; and that is why some people have seen it as offering no more than secularizations of the old ways of thinking and the old answers. It wasn't that; but it could look like that, and then be criticized for it. The same thing happens when Darwinism is criticized as being 'only a theory', and therefore as falling far short of the certainties of faith. A Darwinian controversialist then obliges the critics by dressing Darwinism up as being just about certainly true, but finds himself attacked by the very same opponents for being 'dogmatic'!

In support of Löwith's way of interpreting modernity, one might perhaps cite the Marxist philosophy of history, which does look very like a secular retelling of the old Jewish-Christian philosophy of history. And in support of Blumenberg's point of view, we may quote great figures such as Bacon and Descartes who loudly publicize the radically new beginning they are purporting to make.

Blumenberg's chief objection to Löwith is that in the biblical salvation-history the glorious end of history is brought about by the supernatural intervention of God, whereas in the modern working-class salvation-history the Revolution and then the building of socialism, followed by the arrival of the final communist world, comes about by the working of purely immanent historical forces. Blumenberg thinks the two stories entirely different. But, as we saw earlier, both in the religious myth and in the Marxist history, the Good Time Coming is *simultaneously* a certainty for true believers and something that they must fight for by committing their whole lives to it. In both cases the triumph of the great good cause is certain, but you must also work very hard to make it all come true – which makes the two cases seem much more alike than Blumenberg allows.

The same thing happens in the case of Blumenberg's own theory of modernity. The pioneers of the early modern period – men like René Descartes – did indeed put on a great show of making an entirely fresh start and finding a new way to knowledge. But Descartes was also a careful student of Augustine and Aquinas, and he hoped that in the future the Church might in effect canonize his philosophy as the one most appropriate for Christians in the new age of science. In philosophy just as much as in painting or poetry, those who pass themselves off as the most daring innovators are often the very ones who are the most steeped in the old tradition and still paying some tribute to it.

So what then is different about modernity? We should be suspicious of any great story about modernity, whether it be a Fall-story that tells of a sinful rebellion against God, or a story of liberation that tells how the light of Reason has gradually freed people from the darkness of superstition. Instead we should recite all the old themes, and say that the transition to modernity obviously did involve great dissatisfaction with much in the old religion, a move to a more human-centred outlook, a desire to affirm the values of secular life, a comprehensive critique of Tradition, and the gradually more thoroughgoing application of critical thinking to all spheres of life. But the changeover was slow and gradual, and many people – including some of the greatest – resisted it all the way. To give rough but broadly accurate dates, the consensus of the best philosophers, the toughest-minded and most independent people of all, did not clearly and finally break with Christian dogmatic orthodoxy until the early eighteenth century, and with belief in God until the very early nineteenth century. The break was so difficult that the very people who were making it could not help simultaneously half-veiling it. Thus Locke, Clarke and Newton all try to play down the extent of their own dogmatic heterodoxy, and a century later Hegel similarly writes a historicist philosophy that both seals and tries to defer the Death of God.

Modernity is tough. It is not an ideology, but something more like a process or a fate that has been overtaking us for centuries. Straightforward enthusiasts for it have always been few. Most people have accepted it only reluctantly, as something that is coming upon us whether we like it or not.

What about the currently influential story about modernity that was first told by Nietzsche, and more recently has been adopted by certain neo-conservative theologians? They have argued that philosophy (or modern philosophy, or Descartes' Method of Universal Doubt, or, more exactly, just *critical thinking*) eventually leads only to nihilism. The argument is simple. It is that for the truly critical thinker, everything is dubitable and nothing is sacrosanct. Everything is, as they say, *on the table*, or negotiable. The critical method is indeed both hugely powerful and at the very heart of the Western enterprise. It produces human beings, knowledge systems, political systems, value systems and art styles that are continually subject to critical reassessment and piecemeal reform – with, in addition, occasional major reconstructions. Liberal-democratic politics is a good example of what happens to an important area of culture when it becomes consistently critical: it is not an ideology, but a continuous *process* of scrutiny and piecemeal reform which is literally end-less. It never reaches a conclusion. It goes on forever revising itself, reforming itself, questioning itself.

Critical thinking is then not an ideology but an end-less process, like deconstruction. For it nothing is fixed or entrenched. Which means that critical thinking cannot ever reach a final and categorically true theory about what is real, what is true, and what is good. The critical thinker travels very light indeed: he or she must in the end be a nihilist. And our neo-conservative theologians maintain (rather than argue) that nihilism is a very bad thing indeed, so bad that any way of thinking or line of thought that 'leads' to nihilism must be rejected. Modern (or perhaps rather, postmodern) people are currently being told that their culture has been on the wrong track for centuries. Philosophy (which in effect means 'unassisted human reason') cannot save us: only revealed religious truth, accepted dogmatically, can save us by providing thinking with a sure, divinely given and objective starting point.

We notice that according to this line of argument modernity is not in the least Christian: on the contrary, it is the condition of a culture that is in slightly hysterical flight from religion, a lost and potentially damned condition.

I object. The neo-conservative dogmatists who put forward this argument are clearly people who have never seriously and personally committed themselves to the sustained and thoroughgoing practice of religion. For the practice of religion involves one in a sustained effort of self-examination, and a strenuous pursuit of personal integrity, that over the long years gradually demythologizes the believer. Believers see more and more clearly that their own 'Faith' is just a stack of metaphors, laid down with one layer above another. The metaphors move our emotions and encourage us to action; but what is behind them all: what are they metaphors *for*? When challenged, people will sometimes affirm to me that they think there really is something *there* – where? Beyond, or on the far side of the metaphors. But what *is* this 'beyond', and how do the metaphors succeed in telling us something about it? Nobody can say, of course. In practice, almost all my lifelong friends will confess themselves to have become thoroughly demythologized by the long years during which they have always interpreted religious dogmas ethically and have never actually had occasion to give them real and intelligible *descriptive* meaning. In short, realistic interpretations of beliefs go rusty and fade away for lack of use.

Along such lines as these the end of the religious life for all of us is nihilism, as the great mystics indeed say. The most serious Christians – all of them – eventually go beyond their own faith. One 'sees through' it all. The images are only human images: helpful, but leaving us with no way of knowing how they can be informative. But the Nothingness to which the religious life always leads us can be interpreted in at least three very different ways. It may lead us to depression and pessimism, and talk of 'the dark night of the soul'. Or it may lead us to argue that beyond the images there is not anything, not even nothingness, because the images (of course) have no beyond – an argument that leads us to the realization that our language has no outside, and our life has no outside. There is only the dance, and we rebound back into simply saying yes to life while life lasts. There is nothing else: the 'worldlings' were quite correct all along.

And third, we may argue that because God always was supposed to be simple, infinite and incomprehensible, the believer will never be able to tell the difference between God
and Nothingness, or 'Nirvana'. So why not join St John of
the Cross, and choose to experience the Nothing as love in
pitch darkness, the Spiritual marriage, blissout? We can do
so if we wish.

Now we understand that, in spite of what all the neo-
conservative dogmatists say, a profound knowledge of and a
rich response to the nihilism to which year in, year out sustained criticism leads us is central to the Christian spiritual
tradition. The modern West's practice of intense, systematic
critical thinking and its subsequent confrontation with nihilism is, once again, an objectification and a re-enactment
of standard Christian spirituality. What the monk went
through in his cell, we are all of us now going through at
world level. Disorientation, vertigo, giddiness, and sometimes bliss.

A new story about modernity is now coming in focus, and
it is the oddest story you ever heard. The original Jesus was
an almost-secular ethical teacher, a teacher of wisdom.[55]
Being Jewish, he may perhaps himself have clothed his message in at least some of the language of supernatural religious belief. At any rate, in his day and in what was mainly
a very harsh slave society with only a tiny educated elite, his
message could scarcely have survived unless it were cast in
the form of a religion built around his person and his work.
So 'Christianity', like Buddhism, developed as a religion
and in that form lasted 15 centuries and more. But with the
coming of printed books, grammar schools and an urban
middle class it at last became possible for Christianity to
become something bigger than a religion, namely a whole
culture. The process has taken five centuries, but we now
see it approaching completion. The church-type of Christianity still exists, but it is intellectually null, and morally
much less Christian than the culture in which it lingers as a
gauche anachronism. We need not worry about it: the larger

task of interpreting and diffusing Western culture is more interesting and important.

Western culture is an extraversion and an objectification of the main traditions of Christian spirituality and Christian ethics. It borrows freely from all periods of biblical and church history. For example, from the earliest period it takes biblical ideas about 'the Kingdom of God on earth', and recycles them as Liberty, Equality and Fraternity, as anti-racism, and as modern humanitarian ethics. From a later period it takes the monk's strenuous self-examination and his pursuit of moral and intellectual truthfulness, and recycles them as modern critical thinking. It then also borrows from the mysticism of the past ideas about how to deal with the nihilism to which thoroughgoing criticism always eventually leads.

Are we reinstating a Grand Narrative here? Not quite. As a nihilist, I agree that we have no fully independent yardstick by which to measure 'progress' within history. All I am claiming is that the greatest religious traditions are not easily got rid of. They seem to make various sorts of irreversible difference to, or indelible impression upon, the people who have believed them long and ardently. I have described the legacy of Christianity as 'the accumulated indelible'. Even after the ecclesiastical form of Christianity has died, the accumulated indelible remains and continues to work like yeast within the culture. This process is very effective, so much so that post-ecclesiastical Christianity is already much bigger and morally more interesting than the Church ever was.

If you look only at the Church, you can scarcely avoid concluding that 'Christianity' is now just about dead and finally exploded. If you look at the state of Western culture, you will conclude that Christianity lives on vigorously as the world's dominant cultural tradition – and as, indeed, by a very long way the most important cultural tradition that has yet appeared on earth. Much more even than Islam, Western Christian culture looks unsupersedable because of its way of continuously criticizing and transcending itself.

Scrupulosity

I have suggested already that Western culture has, with
astonishing success, taken various features of religion and
extraverted and secularized them, applying them to the conduct of everyday affairs. The upshot is that Christianity,
which until the Enlightenment was a religion, has gradually
become the moral flavour of a whole culture, and is now
almost globalized.

One of these features is the scrupulous, meticulous,
observant, finicky, punctilious, assiduous and indeed
'religious' following of prescribed routines and procedures.
The starting point here is the performance of religious rituals: all over the world complex liturgical calendars of feasts,
fasts, and other holy days are very exactly observed and
complex rituals are performed, and nobody seems to have
any difficulty with the idea that if the ritual is correctly
done, with everything in just the right order, then it works
ex opere operato (just by the doing of the work, as Roman
Catholic doctrine has it). This nicety or punctiliousness
about religious observances is the norm, and is taken utterly
for granted in many a Third-World country where it has
so far proved impossible to persuade people that the same
meticulousness, if applied to a whole range of small everyday matters like maintaining the water supply, or enforcing
the building regulations, would be very highly beneficial to
everyone. No: the fact is that people everywhere take the
appropriateness of *religious* scrupulosity entirely for granted
(it must be done, it must be done now, and it must be done
in the correct order), but they simply hate the thought of

being equally scrupulous about health and safety regulations, or about punctuality, or about the maintenance of
society's infrastructure.

An interesting compromise solution to this problem comes
from Japan, where the making of a good sword involves a
lengthy technological routine. How are people to be persuaded to remember the sequence of forging operations
accurately? Answer, by interweaving the technical procedure with a religious ritual. People always remember how
to perform a religious ritual in the correct order. So they
are taught the whole ritual, and they are taught the associations between each stage of the ritual and the correspond-
ing technical operation; and now they know how to do the
whole thing correctly, with the ritual sequence acting as the
template and aide-memoire which ensures that the technical
jobs are all done, and done in the right order.

This is interesting and amusing, but we are still left with
the intellectual puzzle: Why is it that religion is so much
more *memorable* than anything else? The best answer I can
give is that religious ideas, rituals, teachings and so on are
always storylike, and have the very strong memorability of
the best stories and melodies.

The second feature of religion that has already been
quoted seems to apply only to monotheistic religions. I refer
to the great importance of being scrupulously and systematically self-critical when you examine your own conscience
before God. To attain the goal of the religious life you must
purify yourself thoroughly, which means that you must
be ruthlessly honest with yourself, seeking out and purging every last little bit of error and self-deception. God, it
is said, is holy and all-knowing, and all human hearts lie
open to his gaze, so that you cannot hope to approach God
unless you are inwardly completely pure. There is a simile
in the background here: just as one bad apple may corrupt
and spoil a whole basket of apples, so one unacknowledged
and unabsolved sin is enough to make you quite unfit and
unable to endure the holy gaze of God.

Extraverted and secularized, this religious self-examination becomes critical thinking, and in particular the scientific method. The only way to truth, real truth, is by a thorough and systematic investigation which considers all possibilities, and by the rigorous expulsion of all detectable errors from your system of knowledge.

It is important to stress that the one and only religious way to knowledge that is important here is critical *self*-examination in the search for purity of heart before God. Two-and-a-half millennia ago critical self-questioning was important in the development of religious asceticism, of psychological reflection, and even of philosophy itself. But all other religious ways to knowledge seem quite content to remain firmly non-critical. The custom was and is merely to accumulate and guard Tradition and to treat every bit of it as more or less equally authoritative, without any critical purging. Thus in Christianity the four canonical Gospels were simply added together to produce a 'Harmony of the Gospels',[56] just as your school nativity play to this day adds Luke's infancy narrative to Matthew's, and then throws in a little embroidery for good measure. Before critical scholarship came along hardly anyone had ever said openly that the Jesus of St John's Gospel and the Jesus of St Mark's Gospel are so different from each other that they simply cannot possibly be, both of them, equally and fully authoritative portraits of one and the same man. But that is how it was: traditional religious faith often incorporated conflicting themes and materials, but people seemed not to notice it. At any rate, attempts at critical tidying-up have always been very unpopular. People do not want to have their cherished beliefs tidied up for them, and least of all at Christmas time.

For our present purposes, however, it is sufficient to limit our attention to the penitent and the ascetic who undertake a scrupulous, rigorous self-examination in the quest for inner truthfulness, or purity of heart. In the background is the awesome, terrible figure of an infinitely holy and demanding heavenly Father, who sets us the very highest standards. We are trying to do his Will by meeting his demands – and there I hope the reader may already have thought of two of the greatest figures in the history of science, Isaac Newton and Charles Darwin. Newton, a *posthumous* (i.e. a child born after the death of his earthly father, like Sartre), was highly conscious of a special relationship to his heavenly Father; and Darwin, in his correspondence, gives a strong impression of one who is trying to live up to the exacting standards set him by a very strong earthly father. Both men, in their different ways, give some indication of the religious background and the psychological cost of the scientific method. Religious, and even perhaps neurotic, scrupulosity is turned outwards so that it becomes *intellectual* scrupulosity – with startling results. Suddenly, we have a hugely powerful new tool.

Compare a traditional *Herbal* with a modern *Flora*. The *Herbal* follows the same pattern as the Harmony of the Gospels, by simply piling up everything, good or bad, that Tradition supplies. So the *Herbal* will typically list all the names of a plant, supply a picture of it, describe its medicinal virtues and its astrological affinities, cite all the references to it in classical literature, and so on until it has supplied several pages of jumbled, miscellaneous information.[57] The modern *Flora* is quite different. It cuts out all the literary references, the folklore, the astrology, the medicinal properties and so on, and sticks strictly to botany. There is a careful technical description designed to help the field botanist to identify the species accurately. There is information about habitat, distribution and abundance. Here we note that, above all, the modern *Flora* contains no errors. The *Herbal* is an antique shop, a jumble of bygones, with almost none of its statements ever having been publicly tested, whereas behind the *Flora* there is a really stringent ethics of knowledge. Quite simply, neurotic scrupulosity, extraverted and applied to the construction of systems of knowledge, has proved hugely powerful. So much so that modern Western natural science is far and away the best and most powerful way to knowledge that human beings have ever devised.

Darwin's biography well illustrates the main points. As eventually published, *On the Origin of Species* (1859) took the form of a lengthy cumulative argument worked up in considerable detail and over many years. In the nature of the case, much of what Darwin was proposing could at that time neither be modelled mathematically nor tested experimentally.[58] He was attempting something like a Baconian induction, and he saw clearly that everything depended upon the facts being reliable, and all the arguments carefully considered. Darwin was diligent in reading expositions of the 'Design' explanation of adaptation, and in reading the relevant philosophers.[59] In his letters he is collecting all the relevant facts and arguments he can get, and he specially thanks people for sending him facts and arguments that appear to tell *against* his theory. He really needs to be made aware of, to weigh, and to deal with every possible objection to his theory before he publishes it.

Darwin took such pains over his great work that one readily understands his invalidism. His anxiety was very high and he clearly shows us the connection between traditional religious and moral scrupulosity (anxiety about one's own purity of heart and motive) and modern Western intellectual scrupulosity.

The history of Western intellectual standards and their progressive refinement over the last few centuries is scarcely yet written; but one day it will be written, and it will be very instructive. Two centuries ago, and even more recently, it was sufficient for a medical pioneer to test a new medical procedure upon himself and a new surgical procedure on his patients. Today, it costs around one billion US dollars to develop an important new drug and bring it to market, because field trials have perforce become so large-scale and expensive.

In these reflections about religious scrupulosity and its transfer into various secular contexts we have learnt something about the religious significance of modern Western culture.

First, in the modern state the old distinction between the secular and the sacred realms has been transformed into the distinction between private life (in which you may, and indeed *should*, put first the interests of yourself and your own family members) and public service (in which you must disinterestedly follow prescribed routines to the letter). The public servant is an administrator, or in Greek, a 'deacon'. The public realm is like God, those who work for it are 'civil servants' or 'ministers', and the highest standards of impartiality or disinterestedness are required. Interestingly, the Greek word liturgy (*leitourgia*) means *both* public service *and* the worship of the gods. Both require the same 'religious' punctiliousness: you must be a 'stickler', an interesting old word with a long history.

Second, modern Western culture depends upon knowledge, knowledge acquired by critical method, and tested by critical standards that are themselves also subject to continual critical assessment and reformulation. A particular tenet or assertion counts as part of the body of public knowledge if it is currently accepted as such by the relevant learned society, is taught in the universities, and is acceptable from an expert witness giving testimony in a court of law. And as we have found earlier, there is an exact analogy: just as in medieval Christian piety the believer was required to carry out a stringent and comprehensive self-examination to make him fit to stand before God, so in modern Western culture any candidate for the status of being public knowledge must be capable of surviving stringent and comprehensive critical testing before it can be deemed fit to stand in public.

Third, not only does modern Western culture give great religious significance to the public realm and public service, but also its commitment to critical thinking and testing requires it to be a continuously self-critical and self-reforming type of society, which is all the time reviewing and developing what it counts as being public knowledge and publicly established values. Unlike any previous culture, modern Western culture since the Enlightenment has attempted continual moral self-criticism and self-improvement by legislation. We have tried to make ourselves morally better by reviewing and raising our public standards for the treatment of prisoners, of the insane, of slaves, of serfs, bonded workers and day-labourers, of animals, of children, of wounded soldiers, of women, of racial minorities, of sexual minorities, of the disabled and many other groups. The Western state has become ethical; it actively works to improve the moral standards of the population, and to this extent the modern Western state remains highly Christian, even *after* the Death of God and *after* the end of the Church. There is much more Christianity around now than ever there was in the Ages of Faith.

Fourth, and lastly, it is worth pointing out that the modern world *expects* Christian standards of the West. People in the poor countries expect the West to feel rather guilty about being so rich, and to acknowledge a duty to 'redistribute' its surplus wealth. They expect the West to acknowledge the sinfulness of colonialism and the slave trade, and to disburse annual development aid, humanitarian aid, and (nowadays) even reparations. They rather expect the West to go on about individual human rights, about democracy and the rule of law, and so on. In short, the rest of the world has a great range of moral expectations of the West, and tries hard to exploit them. But the poor countries don't have the same expectation of other religions and culture-areas. Nobody seriously expects the Turks to apologize to the Armenians, or the Egyptian Arabs to repent of their long domination of the Copts. Nobody expects Indians to dwell on the evils of the Mughal Empire as much as they dwell on the evils of the British Empire, or the Zanzibaris[60] to demand repentance and reparations for so many centuries of slave-trading in *dhows* down the East African coast.

In short, the world assumes that the West is Christian at heart, and that it is much more susceptible to moral appeals, arguments and even blackmail than is any other religion or culture-area. The world assumes (rightly, it seems) that Christian values do still greatly influence Western behaviour. Many commentators assume that Christianity is a dying faith, whereas Islam is very much alive. Because other faiths and cultures show absolutely no inclination to be self-critical in public, they can confidently assert their own moral superiority and the West's relative decadence. But are rich oil sheiks apologizing to black East Africa for slavery, and offering aid without strings? Seemingly not, despite the fact that almsgiving (*zakat*) is one of the Five Pillars of Islam. On the whole, the world notes that only the West, along with some institutions created by it such as the UN and the great humanitarian charities, still takes religious values sufficiently seriously to be persuaded to give money and personal service, unconditionally and on a large scale, over many years, to the needy.

Again I am led to the view that Christianity is doing better in its afterlife as 'Western culture' than ever it did as a religion – if you will allow me to reckon an organization like Médecins sans Frontières as belonging to the history of Christianity.

11

Critical Thinking, God and Nihilism

I have been arguing that of all Western values and traditions the most important and powerful, and the one that we should be prepared to fight for, is the great tradition of free critical thinking. This style of thinking has the effect of keeping all our established – and normally *un*questioned – assumptions, beliefs, standards, institutions and values in a state of being permanently open to questioning and, perhaps, correction. Everything in our collective head that we normally take utterly for granted needs to be able to come out into the open and justify itself. It needs to be able to show that it is of use, is doing a good job, and deserves to be kept – at least until we can replace it with something better.

This critical type of thinking leads us to hope that we can continually question, reform and so improve not only ourselves, but also our social set-up, our ideas about morality, our systems of knowledge, and even perhaps our religions (well, why not?). It opens up the possibility, classically adumbrated by the Elizabethan publicist Francis Bacon, of steady future 'advancement' on all fronts – and Bacon was careful enough and clever enough to link critical thinking with the old biblical and early Christian polemic against idolatry. To liberate men's minds, we must destroy 'idols' of many different sorts.[61]

Critical thinking has indeed proved enormously powerful. Since its beginnings four centuries or so ago, it has progressively emancipated us from Tradition. It has steadily demythologized our whole picture, both of the world and of ourselves. It has given us scientific method, the critical historical method, and humanity's first large and powerful systems of tested knowledge. It has given us the modern, continually self-criticizing and self-reforming liberal-democratic type of society, and finally, it has given us our new culture-heroes, a canon of 'strong', creative, independent writers, artists and thinkers. Today there are dozens of states in which for the first time in history the mass of the population have an excellent chance of living tolerably fulfilled, full-length and culturally rich lives in reasonably good health.

It is hardly surprising that much or most of the rest of humanity want to jump on the bandwagon as soon as possible, whether by migrating to the West or by developing their own countries along Western lines. And why not, indeed? Unfortunately, there are various widely felt difficulties and objections to my line of argument so far; and unless I set them out clearly, and deal with them at length, I haven't a hope of carrying you with me for much longer.

First, if the achievements and influence of critical thinking are so very great, why is it that in some of the leading countries – including the USA itself – most people remain deeply suspicious of it? Why is the world's leading scientific country also the most anti-Darwinian country? This is important, because the movements in various cultures and contexts that are loosely labelled 'religious fundamentalism' are inspired above all by dislike of critical thinking and fear of what it may be leading us to.

Second, is not critical thinking associated with excessive Western individualism, consumerism, populism and hedonism – and so with the great breakdown in the West of traditional moral controls upon the behaviour of ordinary people?

Third, is not critical thinking just like capitalism in being hugely powerful and potentially destructive unless it is carefully regulated? The most publicized apologists for free thinking have always demanded *unrestricted* liberty of thought and expression. But surely that is exactly what they must *not* be given, for unfettered critical thinking, by de-mythologizing everything else and finally consuming even itself, must clearly lead to pure nihilism and cultural collapse. Nietzsche and Jean Baudrillard have both argued as much very forcefully.

Fourth, how can I reasonably claim that the biblical and Western Christian tradition itself, even more than Socrates and the academic sceptics, was the true parent of our modern critical style of thinking, when the Church has always stood for metaphysical realism, for dogma, and for belief upon authority? Surely the free thinkers in every age have been given every reason to perceive the Church as the *enemy*, and not the friend, of intellectual freedom?

In response to this comprehensive fourfold charge, my main arguments so far have been two: one has been the traditional argument of radical theology since Hegel, to the effect that Christianity is the religion in which God really does become human and dies. Over several millennia the human race gradually moves forward from a dogmatic or fundamentalist and God-centred world-view in which God alone is the absolute Judge (or critic: 'critic' is simply the Greek word for judge) of everything, to a human-centred world-view in which *we ourselves* are the only judges of all things. The Bible itself foresees and sometimes anticipates this evolution, for example when it pictures God as beginning the handover to humanity even at the creation of Adam, by inviting him to name the beasts.[62] I have often myself quoted memorable phrases such as "'I said, you are gods'",[63] and Jesus' question, 'Why do you not judge for yourselves what is right?'[64] – that is, be *critical* about morality! In another equally radical saying, Jesus declares that 'The sabbath was made for humankind, and not humankind for the sabbath',[65] which very commendably anticipates the Sea of Faith doctrine that we must get used to the idea that our own religion is only human. Do not fetishize it: treat it merely as a manmade tool, useful today but perhaps to be discarded tomorrow. So I have been suggesting that a modern theologian must read the whole history of the Western intellectual tradition as a long story of the old God's gradual handover of his powers to human beings, a story of which the thinkers of the Enlightenment – such as Kant – saw the culmination, the coming-of-age of humanity, as happening in their own times.

My second main argument has been that much of modern Western thought is simply an extraversion, or turning inside-out, of Christian spirituality. The monk scrupulously and systematically examined himself, trying to purge his own soul from error and self-deception, and pursuing an ideal of purity: the critical thinker scrupulously and systematically examines all our commonly held beliefs and assumptions in order to try to purge away the errors in our stock of public knowledge. Extraverted, the monk's anxious scrupulosity becomes a tool of very great power in the construction of empirical knowledge. On principle, we should doubt everything, test everything, and check the internal coherence of it all.

Now we need to develop a third argument: critical thinking in modern Western culture is the child of the ancient polemic against idols, the negation of images, and the *via negativa* in Christian spirituality. The great mystics always said that the religious life is a journey into absolute darkness and nothingness. Of course it is, and modern critical thinking's journey into nihilism is simply a recapitulation of the same old journey, the Purgative Way. God is the desert, the void, darkness and pure freedom. Haven't you noticed? For the religiously serious person there is in the end no difference between theism and atheism. The spiritual journey, even in orthodox teaching, is a journey into darkness.

The story begins with the sharp polemic against idolatry in ancient Judaism (Isaiah 44.9–20; note also 46.1–2 and Psalm 115.3–8). People are foolish when they allow

themselves to become enslaved by objects that they themselves have made. This line of argument was the standard starting point for the preaching of Christianity to the
Hellenistic world in the first two centuries after Christ,[66]
and it clearly foreshadows Kant's Copernican revolution,
on which modern philosophy has been founded. We want to
see the world and ourselves as being constituted and ruled
by great world-ordering and world-controlling principles,
but it is our own 'objectifying' or 'idolatrous' thinking that
puts those principles out there, for we have to see the world
in terms of them in order to be able to see an ordered and
intelligible world out there at all. To make the same point
in a more recent vocabulary, we can free our thinking from
being ruled by fictions if we can learn to see that much that
we have considered to be natural and unchangeable is in
truth merely cultural, and therefore open to criticism and
to change. We *do* need fictions to think with, but we *don't*
have to be enslaved by them.

When the young Karl Marx read Ludwig Feuerbach's *The
Essence of Christianity* (1841), he assimilated its projection
theory of religious ideas and saw the implications. He was
very impressed, declaring that 'the criticism of religion is the
foundation of all criticism'. True enough, so far as it goes,
but Marx has failed to push the argument far enough back.
He has not acknowledged that religion was the first subject
to become *self*-critical. In the Axial Age great prophets criticized manmade idols and religious images in the name of
an invisible, unknowable Transcendent that was beyond all
the imagery of popular religion, and they launched a sharp
ethical critique of burdensome, manmade traditions and
rituals. That was the original critique. Pushed further by
a line of mystical theologians, the Way of Negation creates
a higher and higher negative theology until it is eventually
forced into non-realism as God eventually becomes purely
ideal. Then, beyond even that, we begin to understand that
the point of the idea of God is its haunting utter impossibility, and we are forced at last to return into time and finitude

and mortality. By being at last seen to be impossible, God gives me back to life.

How does this happen? As the idea of God is pushed higher and higher, at what precise point is God finally pushed out of existence altogether? How does it happen that in the very heart of the religious tradition God must in the end become only darkness, nothingness, impossibility, and perhaps no more than a ghostly memory?

Recognition of the problem here goes back to Plato, but the solution is as recent as the work of Jacques Derrida.

In the *Republic* Plato makes his familiar sharp contrast between two worlds. In the flickering, fast-changing world of time and the senses – the world of everyday human life – our vocabulary is used to refer to fleeting shadows. But if by a happy chance we are delivered from Plato's Cave, and come out into the more real and stable world above ground, the eternal world of ideal Forms, how can we assume that the old vocabulary will still *work*, successfully picking out and describing quite new objects? How can our language, which we developed to serve the purposes of human life down below in the Cave, be adapted to make it fit for a quite different mode of existence in a quite different world?[67]

These questions show how it came about that religious thought found itself confronting critical thinking and 'the crisis of representation' even in pre-Christian times. Even in the later chapters of Isaiah, Greek philosophical influence is already strong enough for the writer to grasp that just as the Holy of Holies in the Temple at Jerusalem was empty and dark, so a journey 'into God' is a journey into empty, image-less darkness. God is strictly incomparable – and there-fore ineffable, beyond language.[68] God's uniqueness and transcendence, as understood by Isaiah, clearly make God *strictly* incomprehensible, empty and unknowable. Plato did not himself 'believe in God' in the strong theistic way, and the nearest he gets to the idea of God is 'the Form of the Good'; but he was quite clear about where his thought was leading him, for Socrates speaks of the Form of the Good as 'beyond Being' – that is, purely ideal.[69] Strange: theism from the first recognized its own atheistic heart.

In the subsequent development of Christian religious thought the *logical* priority of the denial of images, the Negative Way, and the insistence upon the divine emptiness and darkness was upon the whole very consistently maintained until the early thirteenth century, when the Dominican theologians began to develop their doctrines of analogy (i.e. the analogical use of terms in statements about God). After Aquinas, dogmatic theology that serves the power interests of the Church clearly and visibly begins to draw away from mystical theology. The mystics preserve the old, beautiful, and strictly correct pure nihilism – that is, the openness of the soul to pure darkness, void and nothingness at the summit of the religious life – but now, they were liable to get persecuted for it, which is why Derrida has said that the Negative Way wasn't really followed to the end: it was deployed only as a stage on the way to a deeper reaffirmation of God.[70] That's true of dogmatic theology, and of the power-hungry high priests in Rome. But even humble writings in the mystical tradition continued to preserve the truth. For example, Everyman as he goes into death leaves even Knowledge behind:

Everyman	Knowledge, will ye forsake me also?
Knowledge.	Yea, Everyman, when ye to Death shall go;
	But not yet, for no manner of danger.

(Everyman, ll.858–61)

Of course knowledge will forsake him. Haven't you noticed that God is death, God is absolute darkness and nothingness, God is the outsidelessness of life; and that going into death is ceasing to be? There is no knowledge of anything in or beyond death: of course not. But it was hard to say so before modern times: hence the irony that a truth that was clearly implicit in Plato and the second Isaiah could not fully and finally become explicit until Derrida. The whole point of the idea of God is that God is impossible. God doesn't exist and cannot exist. He never did exist, and we have to go all the way in the religious life (guided by someone like St John of the Cross) before we can fully understand our human situation and learn *both* to love life and make the most of it *and* to accept death.

Now at last we learn the deepest lesson about the contribution of religious thought to the meaning of the West. The West's greatest discovery and achievement is its now well-established tradition of free critical thinking. But the free critical thinking which makes us permanently receptive to change also implies that there are no entrenched eternal verities. For the West as for Buddhism, all is 'impermanent'. The Western Everyman must in the end leave Knowledge behind as he descends into the grave. He must learn that there is not, and that there cannot be, anything substantial, unchanging and always present behind the flux of accidents. But of course the West does not go straight into, and flop down in, a state of passive nihilism as being in the end the last and only 'truth'. No – because if pure nihilism were indeed the only and highest truth, there would be no truth, and it therefore wouldn't be true. There is neither truth nor falsity in the grave. So the West cleverly returns us (and always has returned us) into secondariness and the images. The West makes our whole life into a rich and complicated play of images, affirmative and negative, and out of the dialectic between them both builds a world and makes spiritual progress towards the final non-Truth. Critical thinking continually puts forward a construction and a valuation of things, and then criticizes and revises it. It moves continually between affirmation and negation, and so gradually builds up and enriches our life-world *at the same time* as it is also showing us how and why our life-world is outside-less and therefore each individual one of us simply ceases in death.

Thus in the best tradition of Catholic spirituality we see how its dialectic of affirmation and negation teaches critical thinking, builds a complex and valuable life-world, and in the end reconciles us to the transience and contingency of everything – including ourselves. The best Catholic spirituality thus contains in a nutshell the whole wisdom of the West, and the rationale for critical thinking – provided that you will grant me that it does and always did eventually leave 'ontotheology' or 'metaphysics' way, way behind it. Sceptical, self-cancelling Catholic spirituality, which sees that the last truth is that there is no Truth and is content to return into life and secondariness, is the final meaning of the West.

12

The Western Self: Denial and Affirmation

Just about every head teacher in the Western world, when given an opportunity to produce a 'mission statement', can be relied upon to come up with something about the need to treat each child as a unique individual with something to contribute, and about the school's aim to ensure that every child realizes his or her full potential. Et cetera. The school is not a machine that processes children, and it is not solely or chiefly interested in the higher-ability groups. The school acts on the maxim that every child is different, and that there are many forms of excellence and ways to achieve it.

Et cetera. We have heard all this so often: but is it the case that a belief in the uniqueness, the unique value and personal destiny, of each and every human being is typically and characteristically Western? If so, how did this belief originate, and what is its status? Can it be justified?

In the first place, belief in the special value of individuality simply as such is alien to ancient Greek philosophy, and is not found in the earliest Christian writings. For the Greeks in general, and for Plato in particular, matter as such is neither intelligible nor valuable. Value and intelligibility belong only to the world of timeless Forms, which are 'universal' or general, and not particular. An individual human being becomes valuable and (as one might say) *exemplary* only when in one or more of his or her deeds an eternal form becomes briefly manifest in the temporal world – when, as a modern English idiom might put it, he *shows great courage,* and thereby *sets a good example*. Achilles is not thought of as supremely valuable just for being an individual unlike anyone else: he becomes a great example to us only when he comes into a situation that calls for the display of a universal value, and duly exhibits it. The universal briefly reveals itself in time.

What about the analysis of a human being into soul and body, the soul belonging by nature to the eternal world? Aristotle, in particular, is clear that in this case too it is the embodiment of the soul in a material body that individuates us. I am different from you because my body is obviously different from yours. This suggests that if we were both disembodied it would be difficult to tell us apart, and indeed there is a suggestion in the New Testament that naked, disembodied human souls are not complete individuals, and are therefore acutely uncomfortable while they wait to be 'reclothed' in the new bodies that will give them the concrete individuality they need in order to be able to be anything and to do anything.[71]

In short, ancient Greek and early Christian thought were not at all in the business of treasuring each and every human being as uniquely valuable.[72] On the contrary, you became interesting and valuable as an example to others only if and when in your behaviour an eternal, and *general*, moral essence is briefly manifested in the world of time. You become valuable only in and through your relation to the eternal world: such was the background against which people thought that their relation to God, and to God *via* Christ, was quite obviously the most important thing in their whole lives. It was the only route by which human life could gain 'meaning' and worth.

How then *did* the Western Christian-humanist belief in the unique value of even the humblest human individual originate?

It seems to have begun from the idea of a *pleroma*, a complete set, a perfect totality that often needs to include great diversity in order to be complete. Thus the full crew or complement of a ship is a pleroma. In God, the full complement of all God's ideas, 'energies', attributes and operations is a pleroma. And in the heavenly world the whole angelic creation is a pleroma, a vast ninefold hierarchy of angels. Note that in this case of the angels, because of the difficulty I have already mentioned – how can you tell one finite, disembodied soul or spirit from another? – orthodox angelology lays it down that every angel has to be a distinct species. Every angel, therefore, is a unique individual. Like the pieces of a jigsaw, they all add up to a perfect whole.

Now, as everyone knows, the first event in the old sacred history of the created world was the revolt of Lucifer and the violent expulsion of the rebel angels from heaven. This disaster ruptured the pleroma of angels as God had originally designed it. Obviously, the thousands of vacant places in heaven must be refilled, so God created the visible world and the human race in order to get heaven restocked. To make sure that the revolt of Lucifer will not be repeated, God plans to restock heaven with seasoned souls who have lived human lives in time and have successfully proved their loyalty by overcoming the solicitations of Satan. Furthermore, God must fully restore the original pleroma. It follows that the set of 144,000[73] humans who get to heaven must exactly fit the 144,000 different empty slots that await them. It follows that each elect human must be predestined and predesigned for his or her precise slot, and they must all be different from each other.

Such is, I believe, the original context from which liberal Protestant Christianity drew the belief that each and every individual human being is uniquely valuable, and has his or her own unique potential. To the head teacher the school is a pleroma, as the Church is to the bishops. In addition, there are several other uses of the pleroma idea in traditional Christian thought. Thus it was argued in relation to the problem of evil that a maximally diverse world that includes all degrees of imperfection is a better and richer world than a world that is monotonously law-abiding and comfortable.

Aches and pains, sickness as well as health, misfortunes as well as good fortune, a dark side as well as a bright side; all these help to make life richer and more interesting – an argument that apologists continued to use right up to the eighteenth century. In the social world, some Christian apologists have argued that a Garden of Eden populated by a man and a woman was a better, because more varied, world than it would have been if it had contained only two men. (The context for this argument was the need to explain why God, who is perfect, can have created *woman*!) Still in the social world, many people have believed that a class society, being more varied and therefore interesting, is also more *valuable* than a classless, egalitarian society.

All these venerable – and, to tell the truth, somewhat risible[74] – arguments provide the background out of which in relatively modern times it has come to be widely held and taught in the West that every human being is valuable and has a unique part to play in the whole scheme of things.

One other image has made a contribution to these ideas: it is the old comparison between a human group such as the state, the Church or a household and a human body. The body has many members, or organs, and each makes its own distinctive contribution towards the functioning of the whole. The edifying implication is that nobody is unimportant or expendable, and every human being has some contribution to make to society as a whole. It is also important that the whole body lives and *feels* together.

The West's special interest in the varieties of individual human character and personality has also been nourished from some other sources. Early Christian asceticism and penitential disciplines encouraged the attempt to gain self-knowledge and therewith the development of the model of the self as a theatre in which different forces struggle for mastery.[75] All Western psychologies go back in the end to ancient asceticism – to Plato's *Republic* and to St Paul's Letter to the Romans. Second, as the cult of saints grew, it became necessary to distinguish between many hundreds of individual holy persons, each of whom needed to be equipped with an iconography, a simple hagiography, a special area of interest, and so on. Thus the Church taught people to distinguish between hundreds, or even thousands, of distinct individuals, each of whom was or might be of some special religious importance to the believer.

In all, then, the strain of Western moralizing that instructs us to live and act upon the assumption that persons are extremely diverse, that *'it takes all sorts to make a world'*, that everybody is valuable and nobody should be treated as worthless and expendable – this strain of moralizing has a long pre-history in the Western religious tradition. Only in modern times have we begun to take it literally, as can be seen by the fact that only since the rise of modern humanitarianism have people begun to cite it as giving us good reason for never voluntarily terminating any individual human life, whether by abortion, euthanasia, war or capital punishment. Even then, there are limits: we may sententiously declare that 'all life is sacred', but we do not attempt to collect up and preserve every spontaneously aborted foetus, or go on for ever trying to prolong every fading human life for as long as possible. Perhaps the underlying ethical doctrine is merely that we should value human diversity.

This latter doctrine, however, coexists in the Western tradition with the long tradition already discussed of a standard Western type of selfhood, closely linked with the doctrines of sin and of grace, that is variously described by Paul in Romans 7, Augustine in his *Confessions* and *Soliloquies*, and by Luther, Hamlet and Freud.[76] This standard Western self is memorably pictured by Freud as a permanently embattled Ego struggling to cope with pressures and demands on two fronts. From below, the instinctual drives constantly demand the pleasure of being satisfied. From above, the Law (or the internalized Father, God, the conscience, or the superego) continually threatens us with disaster and severe punishment if we give way to temptation. Thus 'the pleasure principle' is perpetually in conflict with 'the reality principle'. It is a very dramatic myth of what a human self is, a tale that has been told in many ways by theorists, and acted out in endless permutations within individual lives. In recent years we have perhaps tired of it and have been wanting to escape from it if possible. But it remains a very persistent story that keeps on coming back to us.

So much for one of the great polarities in Western thought about the self; the polarity between our will to affirm the value of a great – and perhaps endless – variety of different human individual persons, and the fact that we keep coming back to the old standard-model Western self that struggles for ever to reconcile the opposed demands of nature and spirit, the passions and the Law. Notice, too, that this polarity opposes two very different conceptions of morality. When we are talking about the value of individual diversity we clearly have in mind an ethic of self-realization. *Become yourself!* is the watchword: each of us has to find *her own* 'spirituality', *her own* unique vocation, *her own* 'way'. On the other hand, when we are talking about the Ten Commandments, or about the moral law we clearly have in mind a 'natural moral law', a universal law-ethic that bears down with equal authority upon every human being. It seems that in the whole Western tradition, secular as well as religious, different conceptions of selfhood coexist, each correlated with a different conception of what morality is.

Now for a second polarity, that between 'humanism' and 'antihumanism'. The humanist, in this sense of a rather complex word, is a person who follows the ancient maxim *Gnōthi seauton*, Know thyself! The humanist insists that the classical Western individualism, which so many critics deplore, is entirely right. The human self *does* matter, more than anything else. Our first question is and must be: What am I? What is my self: how does it grow and towards what end is it moving? How ought I to live? What must I do to be saved?

A certain anthropocentrism runs through much of the Western tradition. Christianity is perhaps the most anthropocentric of all the major religious traditions, because it sees everything as being for the sake of 'man', circling round him and watching him.[77] The faith's modern turn towards a more vivid sense of self began with Luther and was given a philosophical justification by Descartes. Kant was in many ways sharply critical of Descartes, but in practice the combination of Romanticism with German Idealist philosophy took the self to extraordinary heights in the philosophers J. G. Fichte and Max Stirner. There is a partial parallel to this in English literature, where Wordsworth is well aware of his oddity in following Milton's extremely grand epic *Paradise Lost* with an almost equally grand and ambitious epic about 'the growth of a poet's mind', that is, about himself. But that, for Wordsworth, was how it had to be. Then, after the mid-century, Romanticism over-reached itself and became somewhat crazed. Nietzschian nihilism loomed. The self crashed.

Antihumanism rejects the notion of the self as a self-founding subject that can be treated as being philosophically primary. If you begin philosophy within individual subjectivity, you are sure to find it difficult ever to get *out* of subjectivity and into a common public world. Anyway, where does the solitary, self-founding spirit-self find the materials – the signs – to think with? Surely the self is thinkable only as being secondary. It can exist only as already 'embedded'. It needs society: there must be a larger realm, already shared or common, within which the self comes to itself and learns to function. That larger field is 'language', or 'culture', or just the human social life-world, history. For the antihumanist too much preoccupation with one's own self, its 'interest', its happiness, its destiny, is foolish and damaging. It is 'eudaemonism', and should be avoided. In science, in politics and even in art, it is usually sanest and best to direct one's attention outwards and away from the self.

In religion there is a similar move away from the self. At the earlier stages of religious awakening the standard vocabulary does picture us as being very self-concerned: dissatisfaction, despair, self-examination, the conviction of sin, remorse, contrition, repentance and confession follow – and *then* we are told that the old self-centred self must 'die', and we must be reborn as a new, larger, and more outward-looking Christ-self that lives a new and liberated, selfless, agapeistic life. In short, one of the aims of religion is to free the self from too much concern with itself. (Or so it is claimed: in practice, the traditionally religious are very often acutely defensive and paranoiac in their response to any kind of criticism or opposition.)

To summarize the discussion so far, typically 'Western' ideas about the human self are varied and complex. I have suggested that they can usefully be plotted in relation to two great polarities. One polarity contrasts extreme emphasis upon the value of each unique individual person with, at the opposite extreme, the claim that we all exemplify a single standard model of what fallen human nature is and needs. The other polarity contrasts extreme anthropocentrism of the kind which says that we cannot *not* be anthropocentric because we cannot have any knowledge of anything quite independent of ourselves, with, on the other hand, the objectivism of those who insist that in order to gain genuine empirical knowledge we can and we must forget the self and give our whole attention to the object. 'Externalist' theories of mind particularly stress the way in which the object of our attention 'fills' our thoughts. Thought is like light in that, to be seen, it must *fall upon* something that it makes 'bright'.

Western ideas about the self have then been very varied, swinging between various polarities: diversity versus standard-model, anthropocentrism versus cool objectivism, self-affirmation versus self-denial, 'once-born' versus 'twice-born', and so on; but in this matter of the self the secular tradition of the philosophers and of classical literature, and the religious tradition of the Jews and of Christian writers, are equally complex and have always been interwoven, from the New Testament Epistles onwards. In a word, the secular and the religious traditions are not very different from each other, as we suggested earlier when quoting the case of Bultmann and Heidegger.[78] In this connection, it is worth saying that many secular writers today talk about the religious tradition as if it exists in a sealed-off non-rational world of its own. It doesn't, and it never did. It has often been said of the Jews in diaspora that around the world they have always been ready to take on a good deal of the culture and the thought of the people among whom they happen to be living; and much the same might be said of Christian writers, especially when they are dealing with a topic such as anthropology, 'the doctrine of man', about which there has never been any single, standard, officially defined dogma.[79]

What of the sharp *religious* objection to Western humanism that comes especially from Muslims? God alone should be worshipped, they say, and they deplore any cult of the human image that may seduce the mind away from the invisible Transcendent. They find the humanism of the West – its use of human metaphors such as 'Father' in speaking of God, its doctrine of the incarnation of the 'Son' of God in Christ, and the obvious, indeed glaring, cult of the human in modern Western popular art – all this they find highly offensive. One might say that Islam develops the ancient tradition of Jewish ethical monotheism in a very strongly antihumanist direction: God is the Law, God is pure transcendent commanding Authority. Christianity, on the other hand, develops the same tradition of Jewish ethical monotheism in a very strongly humanist direction: God is with humankind, God has become human, God has poured himself out into the human life-world, and now God is – you may say – 'life'. *Human* life.

At present there is an extremely sharp confrontation between a neo-conservative and ultra-puritan Islamism and 'the West', which it perceives as humanistic to the point of idolatry and as being rotten and ripe for destruction. How do we react to this verdict upon the West?

In the first place, it is obviously true that the West is indeed uniquely humanistic – especially in its liberal-democratic politics, its emphasis upon individual human rights, its feminism (a moral achievement unsurpassed in all human history) and especially in more recent times, its humanitarian ethics.

Second, we have already argued that 'the West' is simply Christianity, and that its contemporary humanism is the product of Christianity's proper historical development. In the eighth century, Byzantine Christians looked rather indulgently at Islam. They did not yet see it as a quite novel and different religion. But second-millennium Christianity grew ever more Christocentric and humanistic, while during the same period Islam was becoming more insistent upon its own radically distinct and antihumanist identity. Now the two faiths have come to seem very far apart. Furthermore, Islam is very clear about its own finality. No further historical development of religion can be envisaged within Islam; whereas Christianity always looked forward, seeking its own future self-transcendence. Jesus was an ethical teacher who envisaged a radically renewed human life-world. He died a violent and premature death, but triumphed posthumously in the Church's faith. The Church, however, always knew itself to be only a temporary stopgap, and looked forward like John the Baptist to being superseded by something greater than itself. Then around 1800 or so the Church died, and it too has been superseded by something bigger than itself, namely 'the West', which is simply radical Christian humanism, and a lot closer to Jesus than the Church ever was. (The story is not yet over, but we should already be thinking about the next leap forward, to something more universal than the nation-state, and something that can live with the thought that human life altogether is perhaps coming to an end before very long.)

Here is a simple formula, to remind us of the dynamic that set the whole mighty historical process in motion. It is a line from St Mark's Gospel:

> The sabbath was made for humankind, and not human-
> kind for the sabbath ...[80]

Whether or not this line goes back to Jesus himself may be disputed: what matters to us is the neatness and the great force with which it states the claims of *both* radical human-ism *and* critical thinking, *at once*. The Old Testament prophet's rejection of idolatry is here generalized into the maxim: Never allow yourself to become the slave of your own ideas or your own institutions. Treat your religious ideas not as dogmas, not as revealed truths, but as tools that will be discarded when they are no longer useful. Critical thinking, radical Christianity, the dynamism of the modern West – it all converges; and now we begin to see what it is that we must be prepared to fight for. Not the Church, be-cause the age of Church-Christianity is over, and we must regretfully abandon the Church. It cannot be reformed now. What we *should* identify correctly is the fundamentally *theo-logical* meaning of the modern West. It is a very late return of Christ: it is critical thinking and radical humanism.

13

The Indelible Dream

Would that all the LORD's people were prophets, and that the LORD would put his spirit on them!

(Numbers 11.29)

On this mountain the LORD of hosts will make for all peoples a feast of fat things, a feast of wine on the lees ... he will swallow up death for ever, and the Lord GOD will wipe away tears from all faces, and the reproach of his people will he take away from the earth ...

(Isaiah 25.6, 8, RSV)

'For you shall go out in joy, and be led forth in peace; the mountains and the hills before you shall break forth into singing, and all the trees of the field shall clap their hands.'

(Isaiah 55.12, RSV)

'I will rejoice in Jerusalem, and be glad in my people; no more shall be heard in it the sound of weeping and the cry of distress. No more shall there be in it an infant that lives but a few days, or an old man who does not fill out his days, for the child shall die a hundred years old, and the sinner a hundred years old shall be accursed. They shall build houses and inhabit them; they shall plant vineyards and eat their fruit ... for like the days of a tree shall the days of my people be.'

(Isaiah 65.19–22, RSV)

'Behold, the days are coming, says the LORD, when I will make a new covenant with the house of Israel and the house of Judah ... I will put my law within them, and I will write it upon their hearts; and I will be their God, and they shall be my people. And no longer shall each man teach his neighbour and each his brother, saying, "Know the LORD", for they shall all know me, from the least of them to the greatest ...'

(Jeremiah 31.31, 33–34, RSV)

'The city shall be rebuilt upon its mound, and the palace shall stand where it used to be. Out of them shall come songs of thanksgiving, and the voices of those who make merry ... Their prince shall be one of themselves, their ruler shall come forth from their midst.'

(Jeremiah 30.18–19, 21, RSV)

'They shall come and sing aloud on the height of Zion, and they shall be radiant over the goodness of the LORD, over the grain, the wine, and the oil, and over the young of the flock and the herd; their life shall be like a watered garden, and they shall languish no more. Then shall the maidens rejoice in the dance, and the young men and the old shall be merry.'

(Jeremiah 31.12f., RSV)

'A new heart I will give you, and a new spirit I will put within you; and I will take out of your flesh the heart of stone and give you a heart of flesh. And I will put my spirit within you ...'

(Ezekiel 36.26f., RSV)

'Behold, the days are coming,' says the LORD, 'when the plowman shall overtake the reaper, and the treader of grapes him who sows the seed; the mountains shall drip sweet wine, and all the hills shall flow with it. I will restore the fortunes of my people Israel, and they shall rebuild the ruined cities and inhabit them ...'

(Amos 9.13f., RSV)

For out of Zion shall go forth the law, and the word of the LORD from Jerusalem. He shall judge between many peoples, and shall decide for strong nations afar off; and they shall beat their swords into plowshares, and their spears into pruning hooks; nation shall not lift up sword against nation, neither shall they learn war any more; but they shall sit every man under his vine and under his fig tree, and none shall make them afraid.

(Micah 4.2–4, RSV)

'Behold, at that time I will deal with all your oppressors. And I will save the lame and gather the outcast, and I will change their shame into praise and renown in all the earth. At that time I will bring you home ...'
(Zephaniah 3.19f., RSV)

'Old men and old women shall again sit in the streets of Jerusalem, each with staff in hand for very age. And the streets of the city shall be full of boys and girls playing in the streets.'

(Zechariah 8.4–5, RSV)

After the battle at the Milvian Bridge in the year AD 312, Constantine the Great became the senior ruler of the Roman Empire, and then after the victory at Chrysopolis in 324 he was universally acknowledged as sole Emperor. It was his policy to establish Christianity as something like the official religion of the Empire, and from as early as 313 disputes within the Church began to be referred to him for arbitration (there being in those days no papacy, in the modern acceptation of that term). Constantine saw that it had become politically necessary for the Church's doctrine to be publicly agreed, defined, proclaimed and enforced, and he accordingly summoned the ecumenical Council of Nicaea in 324. So he created the notion of 'the orthodox faith', defined by the Church itself, politically necessary for the sake of unity, and enforced by the Church authorities with the support of the civil power. Thereafter the struggle to find complete agreement continued for three centuries. It was never wholly successful, but those who count themselves 'orthodox' can fairly say that only two great dogmas of the faith have been defined with some precision, namely the doctrines of the Trinity and the Incarnation.

Out of this history has come a set of assumptions about Christianity: to be a Christian, you must be a communicant member of the Church in good standing, that is, one of 'the faithful', one who holds 'the orthodox faith' as defined by the Church. In effect, faith is equated with correct dogmatic belief, as defined by the law of the Church. Dogmatic truths are held to be divinely revealed, backed by the authority of God and immutable, and they are seen as being something like objectively true metaphysical theories about reality. It is essential for your eternal salvation that you should get them exactly right.

Today, if you stop a thousand people in the street and ask them to state correctly the orthodox doctrines of either the divine Trinity or the Incarnation of God in Christ, you would be very unlikely to hear *one* strictly correct answer, even from a professional cleric. Paradoxically, Christian doctrine has been largely forgotten, while in other respects the West is still battling to entrench liberal Christian ethics in its social institutions and still yearns after the ancient biblical dream of a blessed future world. In the end, it seems that dogmas and creeds do not matter at all, whereas other features of a religious tradition – features that are largely undiscussed – prove to be indelible. They go on constraining us long after we have 'lost our faith'. Of these features, one of the most important is religion's characteristic 'dream'. In the West, the ancient Hebrew prophets' dream of a future earthly Restoration is still alive today both in its Zionist version, and in secular political versions. This is still our picture of the good society, the way we'd like the world to be.[81] Yes, the culmination of ancient Israel's religious hopes is simply secular peace and prosperity for the mass of ordinary people. What else? The prophetic hope was basically 'secular', and in late twentieth-century Western society we saw it effectively realized over large areas of the world – that is, at least in North America, Western and Northern Europe, and Australasia. Alternatively, and a little more cautiously, we are now fully persuaded that it is possible by secular political action, applied science and competent economic management to bring into being the world that the Bible dreams of. And what is this world? It is a world in which the common man sits under his vine and under his fig tree[82] in front of his own house. His wife is herself like the fruitful vine,[83] and he enjoys one of life's greatest happinesses when he sees his children's children, and peace upon Israel.[84] In his time he is so blessed as not to see his life ruined by war, or by plague, or by political oppression, or by famine. That's the dream; and long after Western people have largely forgotten the finer points of Christian dogma they are still battling to secure and entrench, for as many people as possible, the realization of that indelible dream. At the beginning of this chapter we quoted all the principal biblical passages about Israel's hope for the future – a secular hope. It is true that the old prophets did not share either our feminism or our view of homosexuality as an innate condition, but otherwise to a remarkable degree their dream remains ours. And not only ours, for by now it has become the dream not only of Westerners but also of the old 'Second World' of people influenced by socialism and also of many Third-World peoples. A full life, free of the grossest scourges – 'the Four Horsemen of the Apocalypse'[85] – for the common people, or at least, for nearly all of them: it is now attainable, and has already been attained for millions of ordinary folk.

Hegel saw world history as a history of the consciousness

of freedom: 'Once one was free, then some were free, and finally all will be free.' I am suggesting that one may equally see world history as a struggle for the secular and democratic realization of the ancient biblical dream of a restored Israel: a struggle in which some measure of success has already been achieved.

And the general theoretical point that arises from this very brief discussion is that religion's indelible dreams – imaginings of how the moral world we live in might be better – are much more important and durable than religious dogmas. The dreams create a huge and long-sustained momentum, driving us en masse towards their promised fulfilment. A *wall of hope* that propels history.

It is very often complained nowadays that too many of the poor and the disadvantaged have very little aspiration towards a loftier destiny for themselves. They pitch their expectations much too low. Perhaps in future we shall see the social mission of religious people as being not to spread *faith*, but to raise *hopes*, for in the long, long run hope that is tenaciously clung to does indeed tend to be self-fulfilling.

14

The Disappearance of the Sacred

The sacred, as it was historically understood, seems to have disappeared almost completely and finally during my own lifetime. In about 1960 or 1961, as a young parish curate, I was surprised and fascinated to discover that some of our humblest parishioners could never bring themselves to enter the parish church, because it aroused in them uncontrollable feelings of religious awe and dread. In a country church such feelings might have been associated with the churchyard and the dead there buried, but this was a town church with almost no churchyard at all. For the people in question it was evidently the *interior* of the church building that was 'numinous', that is, arousing feelings of religious dread at the presence of a powerful *numen* (a spirit or a god). For people who are religious rather than superstitious, the numinous is usually friendly – awesome indeed, but also fascinating, magnetic, and warm like a great bonfire as seen by a child. But to some of our parishioners the numinous was truly terrifying: to them, as to some individuals in the Hebrew Bible, it could mean sudden death. I was fascinated, because at that time such a strong sense of the sacred was already very rare. What was happening?

In the past, a wide range of different types of location in the natural environment have been considered numinous – many or most rivers and streams, mountain-tops, gorges, dells, caves and storms, especially at sea, together with forests, groves and almost any ancient earthworks such as burial mounds, dykes and henges. Just the feeling that it might be protected by a powerful spirit was sufficient to keep many a burial mound intact until it was first excavated in the nineteenth or even the twentieth century. Today, it is hard to think of any such location anywhere that might still be capable of arousing real religious terror. Many land-scapes remain beautiful and 'uplifting', but none can any longer persuade us to believe in fearsome spirits. The near-est I have ever come was an occasion when I saw a dust devil in a mown English cornfield on a hot August afternoon. A mini-tornado, it presented itself as a spinning column of pieces of chaff, about four metres high, which moved appar-ently purposefully about the field. I was thrilled. I instantly knew it for what it was, but I also recognized instantly that any pre-Enlightenment person would have seen it as a spirit, for this was an exceptionally neat illustration of the way in which scientific theory displaces traditional supernatural belief, and post-science love of nature replaces pre-scientific dread of anything unusual in nature.

The numinous in nature seems to have gone. What about the various cultural objects that are still officially recog-nized as being holy by one's own society? They include sacred buildings, persons, images, rituals, seasons and be-liefs. Among Muslims and Sikhs many objects of this kind do still seem to be regarded as sacred, if one is to judge by the speed and intensity with which they react to any sug-gestion of blasphemy. But here the very fact that the sacred makes itself felt only *indirectly*, and via some people's asser-tion that it has been blasphemed against, is significant. It suggests that *the Sacred can no longer ever become publicly manifest in its own right*. It has become internalized or pri-vatized and is known only by the protective wall of merely *human* indignation that now surrounds it. Blasphemy used to be an offence directly against God, and God punished it with suitable thunderbolts; but today blasphemy is an offence against human religious susceptibilities, and no more than that. With the disappearance of the sacred, blas-phemy has come down in the world.

We see this in our own society, where everything that

once was sacred has now been repackaged as Heritage, and is marketed by the tourist industry. The sacred no longer protects church buildings and they must be kept either guarded or locked. They cannot in Western Europe safely be left open to look after themselves, in the old way. God has left his former 'house', but there does perhaps remain an internalized, or psychologized experience of the sacred among, for example, Evangelical Protestants. These people seem to regard Sunday as a holy day: the men wear dark suits to church, and carry Holy Bibles bound in black leatherette with gilt-edged pages. The barrier between the sacred and the secular has now become a fence within their own psychology, separating the religiously controlled area of their mental life from the secular knowledge and practices by which they earn their crust, and separating lawful, God-approved, married sex from abominable and unclean sexual practices. Their attitudes in certain key areas are often described as 'fetishistic' or 'authoritarian', and it seems that the use of these adjectives points to the strictness with which they feel compelled to police their own psychologies.

From this discussion I draw a dual conclusion. The old objective Sacred, a vivid and even frightening experience of the presence of the Holy God in certain features of the world of experience, is now lost. Only a psychologized or humanized sense of the sacred remains: it causes us to be extremely sensitive to anything that seems to challenge or threaten our inward religious convictions and inhibitions. Demonstrations and even riots can flare up very quickly.

A neat indicator of the decline and disappearance of the old religious Sacred is this. Under the old regime it was *to God* that you felt accountable, and to God that you confessed your sins – even in cases where you had sinned against, and significantly harmed, a fellow human. But in retrospect it seems very odd that when you sinned against your neighbours it was only to God that you confessed your sin, so that even today the standard liturgical forms of words do not direct us to go out and make any restitution to our neighbour. Which is odd, and a modern moral sense finds it offensive that a priest who has sinned sexually with a woman or a child of his parish has for so long been treated simply as one who has sinned against God and against church discipline. The matter was dealt with internally by the church authorities, and the priest was perhaps disciplined, and then moved to another job – but that was all. The bishops who dealt with these cases a few decades ago did not perceive any pressing need to make any sort of restitution to the wronged woman or child. Why not? Because if you really believe in an objective Holy God, all sin is sin against God, and *not* against a fellow human. In a word, sin was a ritual offence against the Holy God, rather than an ethical offence against a fellow human. But today we cannot help thinking that there is such a thing as a sin *against one's neighbour*, and that in such a case one is morally obliged to make restitution of some kind to one's wronged fellow human. Even the church authorities now admit it in cases of sexual abuse. This shows that even *they* no longer believe in an absolutely Holy and objective God in quite the old way.

In this connection, notice that the historical Jesus does seem to side with the modern humanist, rather than with the old believer in an objective Holy God. In various well-known passages – for example his parables, and in 'the Sermon on the Mount' – he puts all the moral weight upon our own 'sideways' relations with our fellow humans, rather than upon the 'vertical' confrontation of Holy God with sinful humanity; and, more generally, Jesus is of course highly critical of then-current ideas about what is clean and what is 'unclean' in matters of food and the like.[86] Broadly, Jesus is 'modern' rather than traditional. He is not an orthodox Christian, nor anything like one. He is a humanist, because for him the essence of religion lies in human social relationships, and *not* in a direct confrontation with the Holy.

All of which makes it the more surprising that as recently as 1917 the German theologian Rudolf Otto (1869–1937) should have had such a great international success with a book called *Das Heilige* (English translation, *The Idea of the Holy*, 1923). In an age when it was at last being admitted that modern theology had failed, and that standard philosophical arguments could no longer make God appear even remotely plausible, a postulated universal human capacity to intuit God directly as 'the Sacred' seemed to open an attractive new way in apologetics. Allied by Martin Buber and the 'Encounter' theologians with various existentialist and personalist theologies, it remained popular until quite recently. But our brief discussion has indicated why people should not have been so enthusiastic about Otto's book. The objective Sacred, *mysterium tremendum et fascinans*, with a very-high-voltage electric fence about it, is an objectionably primitive, violent, anti-human and *anti-ethical* idea. Jesus cordially disliked it, and early Christianity at first was sharply critical of the then current distinctions between the clean and the unclean, the holy and the common. It is very greatly to the credit of Church-Christianity that, centuries later, Pope Gregory I firmly rejected the suggestion that a menstruating woman should be regarded as unclean and unfit to receive Holy Communion along with the rest of the faithful. The best tradition in Christianity does not approve of primitive ideas of the holy and ritual impurity, and never did.

Nor is the Holy any more attractive when it is internalized within human beings, as in the examples from Evangelical Protestant Christianity and Islamic and Sikh fundamentalism that have been cited. Internalized and psychologized, the Holy may make human beings ultra-touchy and liable to sudden outbursts of violent rage – a rage that reflects the violence they have done to themselves.

Where, one may ask, did Otto get his idea of the Holy? From the book of Exodus, surely, together with a few other famous Old Testament passages about the Ark of the Covenant, about the Holy of Holies in the Temple, and so on. But today we increasingly recognize that a text like Exodus was written a thousand years and more *after* the events it purports to describe.[87] Like *The High History of the Holy Grail*, it is a work of fiction, an edifying romance about a very remote ideal past. It was common enough to imagine that 'in those days' (*in illo tempore*) God was much more vividly real to our Fathers than he is to us today. But that was never in fact the case: God never was vividly real to people. There was no Golden Age when religious truth was obvious and easy, and we should not deplore the death of the Holy in recent times. On the contrary, the disappearance of the objective Sacred allows us to see the true excellence of Christianity more clearly. It is a form of religious human-ism, a Utopian ethical vision of what human relationships and human life might become, one day, quite soon. As for Rudolf Otto's book: it was profoundly wrong and mislead-ing. There is no objective Sacred that one might be able in some way to intuit, perceive or cognize.

15

Historical Change, for the Better

In a broad sense, all human societies are and must be traditional; that is, there is in every human society a substantial body of beliefs, customs, skills and values that is greatly prized. It is the people's common 'culture', their 'identity', and it is always passed on to the next generation with conscious solicitude. The word 'tradition' means handover, and is used both for the process of handing over and for the body of cultural material that is handed over. Much emphasis is always laid on the duty to pass it on unchanged.

In tradition-directed societies there is always a highly protective attitude towards Tradition. In extreme cases Tradition is regarded as a sacred plenum. One, holy and complete, it cannot be added to or diminished in any way. This view is common among peoples who suppose that in their religion they are the appointed keepers of a final revelation of divine and saving truth, such peoples including the Sikhs, and great numbers of Orthodox Jews, Eastern Orthodox Christians, and Muslims. To people like these, historical change – and indeed, change or novelty of any kind – is always a threat to which they must respond by cleaving ever more strictly and faithfully to Holy Tradition.

It is not at all surprising, then, that most human beings everywhere have always been strong 'traditionalists', conservatives, people for whom it is always best to stand fast in the old ways, *stare in antiquas vias*. Such people will always try to deny historical change by making a sharp contrast between the superficial level of transient fashion which does indeed present an appearance of continual change year by

year, and the deeper level at which everything really important about life and human nature and the human condition
remains unchanging and indeed unalterable. Thus Tradition
always points us away from things meretricious and fleeting
and towards what is deep and eternal. To that extent, indeed, it is 'platonic': it likes, and indeed it relies upon, the
appearance–reality distinction.

Against this very familiar background – still so conspicu-
ous around most of the world – we may well wonder, first:
How and why does any important historical change ever
succeed in taking place at all, anywhere? Second, we wonder: How did we in the West acquire our modern awareness of living amid continual deep change, going on all
the time? Evidently, 'history' in the modern sense is a far
greater threat to all traditional religious and moral belief
than ever 'science' could be. It undermines all foundations,
and all supposedly unchanging truths. And, third, we may
well wonder: how did the West acquire its most distinctive
and paradoxical 'traditional' belief, namely the belief that
the future can be, will be, better than the past?

Lines of argument already proposed in this book suggest an approach to these questions. Our modern historicism is our sense of the profound way in which historical
periods differ from each other. The age in which you live
shapes you, limiting the range of what you can be and do
and think. And just as *you* are datable, so every human arte-
fact is also a period piece which instantly reveals its date to
the experienced eye. And this historical datability of everything is equally true of landscapes, persons, books, works
of art, items of clothing and furniture, ideas and weapons.
Everything is a period piece, and of course the 'historicist'
doctrine that everything is a period piece is itself a modern-
ist period piece with a strong flavour of the early nineteenth
century. Behind our twentieth-century versions of the doctrine (Foucault, Gadamer, Collingwood, Croce) stand early
nineteenth-century theorists (Hegel, von Ranke, Marx, with
Sir Walter Scott as the pioneer of popular historical novels).

A century earlier again, Giovanni Battista Vico (1668–1744) is commonly regarded as one of the very first to put forward an approximately secular philosophy of historical development through a series of periods or epochs. Then, behind Vico, there is of course the looming presence of Christian dispensationalism in its many forms. The names to quote include Calvin, Joachim of Fiore (1132–1202), Augustine, Irenaeus and St Paul. Finally, at the source of this whole tradition is the Christian Bible itself, and the remarkable extent to which Christian thought and worship have always been a meditation on what is believed to be the greatest single historical change of all, the changeover from the Old Testament to the New Testament, from Israel to the Church, from BC to AD, and from 'the Word of God written' to 'the Word of God incarnate'.

This long pedigree invites the thought that all our Western ideas about history are theological in origin. In the classical Augustine-to-Milton account, the Fall of the Rebel Angels left God with the problem of restocking the eternal world. He created the first human beings – but soon they also fell. So history was next devised by God as a long process of education and a drama of redemption, passing through a series of dispensations, or theologically distinct periods. Gradually human beings would be trained and tested until they were fit for eternity. While they lived in time and were undergoing their moral formation, humans would live embodied lives in historical time; but when their moral and religious formation was complete they would be ready to die, and then to live as immortal souls in the eternal world. Alternatively, they might be re-equipped with new, risen and immortalized bodies.

After Milton's time, history was quickly secularized. We ourselves come to be seen as collectively the makers of our own history, and the old theological dispensations, when secularized, become the new historical periods. The old sense of divine Providence, encompassing us all about, and prescribing everything, is transformed into the new awareness of how deeply we are embedded in and shaped by the particular period in which we live.

But now what are we to say about the West's ceaseless, restless energy? What makes us so *driven*? The old dispensational change was driven by the Will of God, but what is the motor of humanly directed historical change? In the mythical-religious idiom of the biblical tradition, God experiences the Fall of the Rebel Angels, and then the Fall of Man, as a setback and indeed as something like an insult. He's got to put it right: he needs to reconfirm the glory of his own great Name. But we, we humans – what drives *us*? What motivates our restless historical striving?

One of the first modern philosophers to raise the question of a secular philosophy of history was Thomas Hobbes, an admirer of the great pioneer historians of Greece, Herodotus and Thucydides, and also of the new post-Galileo vision of a physical universe in ceaseless motion. Hobbes saw that the traditional orientation of philosophy and of all human life towards the eternal world and timeless truth now needed to be corrected. In his materialistic account of human nature, he pictures us as motivated by an insatiable 'striving for power after power, that ceaseth only in death'. He firmly rejects the old doctrine that the goal of human life is eternal rest in the contemplation of the Highest Good (*Summum Bonum*). Our nature is to be for ever restless and discontented, and this new idea becomes commonplace in the generations that follow. It is prominent even in, for example, Samuel Johnson – a conservative Christian writer – who uses it to set in motion the story of *Rasselas* (1759). It is further given a biological twist by the Schopenhauer-and-Freud tradition of seeing human nature as a bundle of insatiable and often conflicting drives, that urgently demand gratification by coming out into expression in our conduct. If the drives cannot find direct gratification in our behaviour, they may at least obtain relief by finding some symbolic outlet in our utterances, or in our fantasies or dreams.

We do not need to go further by talking of Darwinism

and of the way in which post-Darwinian philosophers such as Nietzsche, William James and Heidegger saw that if a Darwinian view of humankind has to be accepted then it will be necessary to tilt the whole of philosophy away from Platonism and towards pragmatism. That much is obvious, for if Darwin is right then our beliefs must be regarded as tools that aid our survival; but in any case it is already clear that the West's gradual changeover from a theological to a secular and humanistic understanding of history must involve considerable complications. When God was the Lord of history he was not himself caught up in the process that he ordained. He was eternal, outside the story, organizing and directing it towards a glorious conclusion, as he drew events in time towards their Last End in his own timeless Being. But what is it like when *humans* come to seize the reins of history? If they are immersed in their own contemporary period, how are they to know for sure what energies, in themselves and in their environment, they are directing, and to what end? They simply do not have the kind of absolute vision that God used to have when *he* managed everything, and it is not surprising that modern politics usually involves debates and battles between different parties – a party of conservation versus a party of change, a party of liberal idealists versus a party of hard-nosed 'realists', a party of law and order versus a party of free self-expression, and so on. Often, we seem to suppose that liberal democracy is an unending and endless debate between these various parties about what has gone wrong and how to fix it – so that liberal democracy goes on, End-lessly and shapelessly, without ever reaching any grand conclusion. The artistic form that reflects this End-less postmodern kind of politics is the soap opera, which meanders on indefinitely but which may nevertheless succeed in being entertaining, instructive and worthwhile as it goes along. If you are nostalgic for the old order, you may complain that there's no 'point' in the soap opera; it never 'gets anywhere'. But the soap opera may still help us to cope with our own lives; and in postmodernity if you have learnt the trick of solar living you can find or create supreme value just by the way you commit yourself to life in the present moment. Thus a life that is transient and quite without any external End may nevertheless be supremely precious and blessed *to the liver, while it is being lived*. Of course, we must accept that neither we nor the value of our lives can continue after our deaths. But the present, transient blessing, present laughter, may be enough.

The West is strange: endlessly self-critical, restless, innovative, yet never getting anywhere, bittersweet and yet hugely in love with life ... You don't like the sound of it? It's all there is for us, now, and you'd better start getting used to it. And, by the way, it seems to be what the original Jesus stood for. We have come full circle and back to him, after all these years.

16

The Ethical Difference

In St Matthew's Gospel (25.31–46) the Parable of the Sheep and the Goats gives clear and memorable expression to the main themes of early Christian ethics. On the Day of Judgement, we are told, people will be assessed solely in terms of whether they did or did not feed the hungry, give drink to the thirsty, offer hospitality to strangers, clothe the naked, and visit the sick and people in prison. It is very striking that the Church, which later came to stress doctrinal orthodoxy more than anything else, should here have preserved a parable which suggests that Jesus himself was quite uninterested in dogma and cared only for the ethics of human relationships – and especially, for our response to a fellow human in need. But there it is: the Church has always been honest enough to allow the contradiction to stand: Jesus cared only for ethics, and the Church cares only for its own 'regime of truth' – that is, for the connection between doctrinal orthodoxy and clerical power.

In fully developed Catholic Christianity the ethical summary in Matthew 25 was retained as the basis for the standard list of seven Corporal Works of Mercy: they were feeding the hungry, giving drink to the thirsty, clothing the naked, harbouring the stranger, visiting the sick, ministering to prisoners, and burying the dead.[88]

Elsewhere in the gospel tradition Jesus is pictured as giving a list of signs that the long-awaited time of restoration and renewal, the coming of 'the Kingdom', is near. In Luke 4.18 he reads aloud in the synagogue at Nazareth, from Isaiah 61.1, a passage in which the sign of the Kingdom's

approach is that good news to the poor, release to the captives, regaining of sight to the blind, and the retaining of
liberty for the oppressed are now being *proclaimed*; but in
Matthew 11.4–5 (the reply to John) Jesus points to what,
as he claims, is actually being *done*: 'the blind receive their
sight, the lame walk, lepers are cleansed, the deaf hear,
the dead are raised, and the poor have good news brought
to them.' Evidently Matthew is here doing again what he
has done in the Parable of the Sheep and the Goats, namely putting his own doctrinal spin upon the tradition that
he received. He wants to suggest that Jesus is 'himself the
Kingdom': the Lord is put into a supernatural setting, and
seen as embodying his own message. His life is the teaching,
enacted. Venerating him, we preserve his message on ice
until the day when it can be lived on earth. To promise his
'return' is to say that one day his message will be put into
practice. Setting that aside, the passages do add one or two
interesting points to the ethical summary in the Parable of
the Sheep and the Goats, for they say that in the new world
Jesus announces there will be a great effort to heal the sick
and the disabled, and to relieve people weighed down by
poverty and oppression.

Enough: the Christian Church preserved – even if in
veiled form – the tradition of a Jesus who was what we
would now call a strong humanitarian and, some might
even say, a socialist. He did not teach a system of supernatural doctrine: he simply announced the coming of a new
moral world. Instead of their present relations of domination and discrimination, people would learn simply and
directly to respond to any fellow human in need, by feeding, clothing and giving alms, and by generally relieving
poverty and oppression; by visiting the sick and prisoners
and seeking the release of captives; and by hospitably wel-
coming immigrants and other aliens. In short, the world
will be a better place when we can give up the habit of
trying to think up reasons for despising or dominating our
neighbour, and learn instead how to love the 'neighbour',

the ordinary person next to us, and how to live from the heart. That's it. That's all.

In the earliest Christianity there are some traditions of attempts to carry out parts of this agenda. Money was collected, for example, for distribution to widows and 'poor saints'. As their name implies, deacons and archdeacons were intended to do just that sort of social-security job.[89] But the ancient Graeco-Roman world was a very harsh slave society with little interest in humanitarian considerations. Is there a single case of humanitarian prison-visiting in the whole of pagan Antiquity? Did anyone organize relief for the survivors of Pompeii? In a largely pitiless age, it is scarcely surprising that Christianity soon developed into a very other-worldly religion. People became extremely individualistic, to such an extent that it is fair to say that from the fourth to the seventeenth centuries, if a person performed one of the Corporal Works of Mercy he or she did so, not out of compassion for a fellow human, but simply at the command of God and for the sake of his or her own eternal salvation.[90] In the early Christian Empire there was some legislation that was influenced by Christianity – for example, establishing Sunday observance and forbidding infanticide – but on the whole it is true to say that large-scale and efficient collective action to relieve human need of various kinds was not forthcoming from either the state or the Church for well over a thousand years. The overriding religious concern was with securing one's own eternal salvation. For the traditional churchman it was rational to act in obedience to divine Law, but it was *not* rational to act on the basis of mere human feeling. But Jesus' teaching was not wholly forgotten, and especially from the twelfth century onwards many wealthy and powerful individuals and corporations established charitable institutions such as village schools, almshouses for the elderly, 'hospitals' or guest-houses for travellers or for the sick, and so on. England is one of the richest of all countries in such institutions. They kept alive a great and vitally important moral tradition, namely the Christian humanitarianism that derives ultimately from Jesus, in times that in other ways were usually very ugly and cruel.

Today we live in a period when the whole subject of religion in general, and Christianity in particular, is surrounded in many people's minds by acute embarrassment and active dislike. People actively seek to bury and to forget the Christian past, and have become largely unaware of the Christian origin and meaning of modern humanitarian ethics. The Victorians were very well aware of the Christian ethical inspiration of institutions such as hospitals and sheltered accommodation for the elderly, the poor, the insane and abandoned children, and of societies that campaigned for prison reform. But today people have forgotten the history of their own moral institutions.

Interestingly, the Christian humanitarian tradition has continued to innovate vigorously within the voluntary sector, even *after* people have long discarded and forgotten the theology of the Church. Examples of this are many and very striking. The rich in the West have, for nearly two centuries now, donated paintings and other objects to great public museums and galleries, where the general public can view them free of charge. Blood donation and organ donation are of very recent origin and highly Christian – as is revealed by the great difficulty of persuading people whose cultural background is *not* Western Christian to become organ donors. Again, a third example of the continuing creativity of the Christian ethical tradition is the establishment in the West of secret refuges for women who are fleeing from domestic violence, forced marriages and the threat of 'honour' killing. (If, by the way, you doubt the uniqueness of Christian culture's attitude to women, try to find a contemporary parallel to Jesus' attitude to women in any other culture, anywhere.)

Our current public language describes the wide range of moral concerns and institutions that we are discussing as 'voluntary' or 'charitable'. *Voluntas* is free will, *caritas* is

love, and in the equivalence of these terms we have preserved the very beautiful Western Christian bond between
altruistic love and pure freedom. Where else can you hope to
find that particular association of freedom and love? *Where
else?* If you move to a part of the world that is *not* historically Christian, you will soon begin to notice the difference. Are there, for example, women's refuges in the Middle
Eastern countries where they are most needed? Of course
not! City life *minus* the Western philanthropic and humanitarian traditions, *minus* 'charity', is so cold and hard that
you soon begin to realize that almost the whole of what we
think of as humanity or humaneness is Christian. The almost unspeakable truth, the strange paradox, is summed up
in two propositions: none of Christian dogma is straightfor-
wardly just true; and we owe to Christianity, and ultimately
(it seems) to Jesus himself almost the whole of our feeling
about what it is to be fully human, or 'humane'.

Harold Bloom has suggested that it was Shakespeare who
chiefly invented the modern human self. I disagree. It was
Jesus, in his ethical sayings and parables, who chiefly invented the modern human *heart*.

Now we have to consider the still bigger paradox. During the last decades of the seventeenth century the Church
lost its grip, and the so-called 'decline of religion' began
in the West. In the 1670s and 1680s the last battles were
being fought between ancients and moderns, and between
Platonists and mechanists. The platonists included figures
like Ralph Cudworth (1617–1688), author of *The True Intellectual System of the Universe* (1678), arguably the last
full-scale defence of the traditional religious cosmology.
The greatest mechanist was Isaac Newton (1642–1727),
author of the immortal *Philosophiae Naturalis Principia
Mathematica* (1687), and Newton's overwhelming triumph
meant the end of any view of the universe as having objective value and teleology (or purposiveness) built into it. It
therefore also meant, in the end, the Death of God – or at
least, of the realist God, the objectively real Creator of the

Universe. Hence 'Newton, with his Prism and silent Face'[91] – in a quiet way, a terrible line, for Newton and Cudworth were of course both of them ordained and had some intimation of what was at stake.

The generation of philosophers who were flourishing in the period between 1687 and 1725 were the very last generation for whom God was a great public object, a metaphysical reality that was the same for all of them and which they all acknowledged. They were people like Locke, Clarke and Berkeley, and Malebranche, Leibniz and Wolff. They all believed in a God who was already there, a *given*; whereas any later philosopher who wished to use the word God had to construct *his or her own* idea of God *within* his or her own philosophical system. God was no longer objectively *given* and the same for everyone in quite the old way. I suggest then that some time around 1720 or so is perhaps the best date one can set for the Death of God. It is the date when metaphysical theism ceases to be sure, when the Great Tradition of Christian art peters out into the fantasy and illusionism of South German Rococo, and the leading Enlightenment intellectuals begin mockingly to distance themselves from the Church. Deistic literature flourishes. One can make a case for many other turning-points, some much earlier (Shakespeare, or even the Florentine Humanists), and some much later (Kant, Nietzsche), but the early eighteenth century is perhaps the best of all. Readers of Jane Austen may recall from the discussion in Chapter 9 of *Mansfield Park* (1814) that the decline of religion is already well under way. Daily prayers in the chapel at Mr Rushworth's house, Southerton Court, were discontinued in his father's day, and among the present party only Edmund and Fanny take religion seriously. For the others it has become a bore.

If then we take the 1720s as the most convenient date for the Death of God as a great and given public Fact, we will soon remark that the very same period also marks the beginning of the modern philanthropic and humanitarian tradition that has been growing steadily ever since. Thomas

Coram was involved with James Oglethorpe's Georgia in the halcyon days (the 1730s) when it hoped to remain free from slavery, and with Nova Scotia when it aimed to provide a new life for the unemployed. His Foundling Hospital in London (1739) drew together a range of notable sponsors, like William Hogarth who endowed it with money, while others gave their time and their works. Upper-class emotional tourists who visited the hospital were discovering a new morality: instead of being grounded upon rational obedience to published divine Law, human conduct could be motivated just by human feelings of warm compassion and active benevolence. A great historical turning-point: the Death of God and the birth of the human heart by which we live, both at once.

During the later eighteenth and early nineteenth centuries we find that more and more good causes are discovered, and committees are formed to promote them. Among the best remembered are the campaigns to improve the treatment of prisoners and the insane, and to abolish the slave trade. At first, committees of individuals promote a good cause by founding an institution. It might be an orphanage, a school or even a waterworks. But, especially after the French Revolution, what is being campaigned for is a change in the law: that is, the public are demanding that the state itself must become actively humanitarian. The state itself must actively *regulate* the social changes being brought about by the Industrial Revolution: child labour, working hours, public health, trades unions, a national system of education, and so on. The public sphere becomes a sphere for humanitarian initiatives to benefit the common people, and from the 1830s great public museums and galleries are established in the principal cities, to be endowed by the benefactions of the rich. Humanitarian sentiment begins to be extended to animals, and in both Britain and the USA, in the 1840s, legislation against cruelty to animals precedes by some years legislation against cruelty to children.[92]

The whole long history reaches a kind of peak in the

career of William Henry Beveridge (1879–1963), whose reports *Social Insurance and Allied Services* (1942) and *Full Employment in a Free Society* (1944) became the basis for the post-war welfare state, together with the 1944 Education Act and the 1948 National Health Service. Much of all this has spread very widely and rapidly around the world, and has become indelibly a part of what we all now expect from the state.[93] While religion is in precipitous decline, the modern state has become the Christian state!

Today, to a remarkable extent, people the world over expect the state to be the Kingdom of God on earth. At least in the more developed countries, the sovereign Authority in the state is expected not merely to *rule* the people, but actively to look out for and promote their well-being from the cradle to the grave. And this expectation is historically part of the indelible difference that Christianity has made to life, first in the West and now to human beings everywhere.

17

The Afterlife of Christianity

This book began as an inquiry into the meaning of 'the West', and in particular it began with the controversy between those like the present Pope who insist that the Latin Church is and remains the West's central institution, the repository and the guardian of the distinctive beliefs and values that have made the West what it has been and still is, and, on the other hand, those who hold the secular 'French' view that the core values of the modern West stem from the Enlightenment. This latter, secular view of the core values of Western culture is usually presented to us along with hazy claims to the effect that the Enlightenment bequeathed to us great and classical ideas of universal Reason, objective Truth, Freedom, Justice, human solidarity and so forth. All will be well with us in the West so long as we remain faithful to these sound and commonsensical ideas. They will protect us from both the Scylla of religious superstition and the Charybdis of 'postmodern' relativism and nihilism. Or so some say.

In the course of our discussion we soon found reason to be highly dissatisfied with both of these stories about the core values of modern Western culture. Western culture today depends most of all upon the free, critical style of thinking that continuously criticizes and seeks to reform everything including itself; and also upon a powerful tradition of thoroughgoing humanism which insistently reminds us that everything that we are and that we produce is 'only human'. This 'humanism of weakness' makes our knowledge strong by insisting that it is always corrigible, and it makes our

morality compassionate and humanitarian. Both in episte-
mology and in ethics, it brings strength out of weakness.
Aesthetically, it leads us to love everything that is mutable,
transient, 'weak' and shimmering. We learn to live without
eternity, without foundations, and without any kind of absolute knowledge or reality. Instead we are content to love
life and to try to live it to its fullest, so that each of us may
hope to make our own small contribution to the human
world as we pass away. Secondariness and transience are
enough for us.

If the modern West is committed to some such outlook
as has just been described, it will be obvious that the Catholic Church's historical record does not exactly qualify it to
describe itself as the central Western institution. For almost
all its history the Church has been dominated by the professional clergy, extremely greedy for power and fiercely in-
tolerant of dissent. It has taught a religion of other-worldly
salvation which has involved ideas about an eternal supernatural world, and about life after death, that are obviously
untrue.

But if the Catholic 'religious' thesis about the core values
of the West is untenable, the secular, Enlightenment one is
equally so. It is put forward most determinedly by scientific
rationalists and dogmatists who have not in fact studied
any of the major philosophers of the Enlightenment, and
have not noticed that the radical critique of reason, objective reality, truth and so on that culminated in Nietzsche
was already under way in the early eighteenth century.[94]
It is of course quite true that orthodox Western scientific
method is by far the most powerful and dynamic way to
knowledge that human beings have yet found. But many
scientific rationalists ignore the history of philosophy, and
indeed the history of their own subject, and as a result profoundly misunderstand the special character of scientific
knowledge. In brief, the Catholic religious dogmatists and
the Enlightenment scientific rationalists both make the same
mistake. They are both 'realists': they both want to teach us

to believe that the special body of knowledge out of which they make their living is objectively and permanently true. But it isn't, and it cannot be. After Hume and Kant Western thought began to understand more and more clearly that we are only human beings. What we like to call our knowledge is always conditioned by our own human point of view, our own place in history, and the language available to us. Language – and in particular the meanings of words – cannot be held still. Language changes all the time, and we cannot stop it shifting. (Actually, it is the shifting that is exciting, for it reveals to us the continual birth of new meanings and new truths.) And as we begin to understand that human beings and their language are always historically situated and changing, so we see that all values, and truths, and even reality itself are always shifting and sliding.

As Western thought has grasped the implications of all this, it has been compelled to move from the old dogmatic realism to a new and more pragmatic notion of truth.[95] Our truths are the fictions that help us to survive.[96] They work today because they help us to find our way around and to accomplish our purposes; but tomorrow the human situation will be somewhat different, and we will need new truths for that new situation.

Very well: but if it is so obvious that for us humans all being – and therefore all meaning and value and truth – is temporal, why was the realist error ever made, and why are there so many backwoodspersons still clinging to it? There are two main reasons. The first is that realism greatly strengthens the claims to power of the body of professionals that teaches it. The priests, or the scientists, can assure themselves that the body of knowledge to which they owe their status is objectively and permanently true. It will keep them in business. And the second reason, related to the first, why realism is so seductive is that people cling so hard to the belief in a *cosmos*, a real world, ready-made out there and prior to us, which is already in working order. It has a system of physical laws which it is already obeying, and a

system of 'natural moral law', a moral world-order with objective values already built in. And this whole ready-made
and furnished house, with everything plumbed in, switched
on and working, was sitting there waiting for us humans,
long before ever we came along to occupy and take posses-
sion of it! Why do people believe such stuff? Because they
have somehow supposed that the Creator might disappear,
or cease to be believed in, while yet the creation that he set
up for us could continue to be there, *unchanged*! Idiotically,
many people forget that not only God the Creator, but also
his creation, is an object of credal belief. Give up the former,
and you must logically also give up the latter, and recognize
that without God's creative activity holding it all together as
a cosmos, the world instantly collapses into chaos.

For this very reason, many of the thinkers of the Enlightenment (and especially the most politically minded ones)
clung on for as long as they could to a shadowy notion of
God; for they saw that God was still needed, even in the
new secular humanist age, to hold the law-abiding world
together. That's why the word 'God' is still printed on the
dollar bill. (The dollar is now off the gold standard, but its
value is still upheld by God.) But at the same time stronger
thinkers such as Hume and Kant began to develop new
theories about how we, *we ourselves*, are able out of the
formless, jostling chaos of raw experience to construct a
cosmos, a habitable world for ourselves. At the same time,
many of the moralists of the Enlightenment also struggled
to develop new theories of a purely human basis for morality, finding it for example in human sympathy, in feelings of
benevolence, or in feelings of personal pleasure and pain.

Thus during the Enlightenment period and afterwards,
a long line of thinkers set about the huge and very difficult
task of replacing the old theism with the new humanism.
In the old order, God created the world, and imposed the
Moral Law upon us; but in the new age it is increasingly just
we ourselves who, within our conversation, are continuously building, criticizing and rebuilding our common picture

of the world and our common values. But note the difference: whereas God created *the* world, we can make only
our world. In time we next come to see that it is also within
our own conversation that we are constructing and revising
our stories about what we ourselves are, and indeed, what
language is. Then at last, through this insight, which I call
'empty radical humanism', we begin to grasp that there is in
the end only the dance of language. With this, we come full
circle: we take up the sententious biblical line, 'In the beginning was the Word', and we rewrite it, 'In the end, there is
only our language.' The dance – or rather, *this dancing* – of
language is the only universal matrix, within which everything comes to be and passes away.

With this glimpse of the End of Western thought, we can
now return to the question of the meaning of Western culture. Having given up both religious dogmatism (the Ratzinger answer), and scientific rationalism (the 'French', Enlightenment answer), Western thought since Nietzsche has
tended to take the view that the central theme of the whole
Western tradition has been critical thinking, consistently
followed through all the way to nihilism (or 'empty radical
humanism', or 'there is only this dancing of language') in all
areas of life: not only natural science, but also history, religion, philosophy and ethics. In all areas, critical thinking
leads us to see that our vision of Nature is always shaped
by our culture: things look the way they do because we
think the way we do. Faithful to this principle of free critical thinking, Western thought is perpetually self-criticizing
and self-reforming, and also dynamic and productive to a
degree that is without parallel elsewhere.

Many people fear and suspect that we have entered into
a Faustian bargain, but they are wrong. The bargain is this:
you can have the joy and the freedom of critical thinking,
the huge extent and power of modern science and technology, and the shimmering, flickering beauty of transient phe-
nomena; you can have all of that, but you must accept that
everything has become ultra-light. You must forget all talk

of absolutes, certainties, ultimates, pillars, foundations and eternal things. Instead just love the dance, for it's all there is. And of course stick loyally to reason, critical thinking and scientific method. If you don't like the bargain I'm sorry, but collectively *we have already made it*, and there is no turning back now. Some people do of course try to turn back – but there is no answer in that direction, and they will only find themselves getting into worse and worse difficulties.

The Meaning and End of the West is then a kind of nihilistic and highly creative religious humanism that loves life, finds secondariness utterly beautiful, and accepts transience. Just love your neighbour and live as affirmatively as you can until you drop. The bargain we have made will deliver quite sufficient prosperity to us; it can give to nearly everyone the best life we humans could ever reasonably hope for; and it is all there is. We have already chosen this option irreversibly, and it is (as I have been arguing throughout) the long-awaited Kingdom of God on earth. This nihilistic religious-humanism-for-a-world-that-knows-it-is-passing-away was, very probably, and so far as we can tell, the original message of Jesus.[97] He came to a dreadful end. His followers – perhaps reasonably – were unable to see how his new vision could be realized in the then prevailing conditions, unless he were to return. So they took the, then obvious, line by exalting him to heaven and declaring him the Messiah-designate. He became a cosmic figure, himself the symbol of the world that he would return and establish here, one day. Meanwhile a disciplined army of his followers was formed under the leadership of the successors of his first disciples. They met regularly, communed with him, remembered his message and called upon him to return: *Maranatha!*[98]

The eschatological hope, that one day the Lord would return and everything would be fulfilled, persisted in the new religion (Christianity, as it came eventually to be called) and became a powerful internal drive within the Faith towards its own *self-secularization*. Faith desperately wishes

to see everything above us come down to earth, and everything hidden made manifest. A plenary incarnation of God
in humanity (that is, technically, in *generic* rather than *individual* humanity) has already taken place: thus Christianity's central dogma functioned as an 'earnest' or guarantee
of the whole programme's completability. And so strongly
was the desire for religious immediacy felt that as soon as
Christian culture in the West relaxed just a little and began
to look with a slightly more friendly eye upon this world
and upon human fellow feeling – I'm talking, of course,
about the late twelfth century – the self-secularization of
Christianity began, hesitantly at first, but gradually more
and more strongly, though the long process does not become fully conscious of itself and of its own meaning until
after Hegel, a full six centuries later.

We Westerners clung fiercely to the religion of Christianity, almost without exception being very reluctant to make
an open break with it. This was true of Kant and Hegel, and
it remained true very recently of Heidegger, Wittgenstein
and Derrida. The greatest philosophers have still looked
back nostalgically to religions – whether Jewish, Catholic or
Lutheran – whose ways of thinking are by now at least three
centuries out of date. This book has expressed my own feeling that I can at last finally leave the old religion behind, not
just because what is left of it has now become so weak and
irrational, but much more because the afterlife of Christianity has now become so much bigger and more interesting
than its earlier period of existence as a great world religion.
The British Labour Party, for example, has done far more to
build the Kingdom of God on earth during the past hundred
years than the Latin Church achieved in the same territory
during the whole millennium AD 600–1600.

Christian supernatural doctrine has not been public
truth for centuries. Jane Austen, for example, is a profoundly Anglican novelist. In her world clergymen abound,
and many of her characters are very serious about religion.
Christian ethics – at least in the form of an acute aware-

ness of and sympathy for the feelings and the misfortunes of others – is everywhere presupposed. But nobody in the entire Austen canon seriously advances a proposition of revealed theology, or even so much as mentions the name of Christ. We cannot imagine any of them doing so. In brief, even in Jane Austen's world Christian theology is already dead. The Anglican Church is still around, but Christianity is in reality already well into its afterlife period. Perhaps something similar might also be said of Daniel Defoe and the later eighteenth-century novelists. And certainly something similar may still be said of today's senior Labour Party figures. Tony Blair and Gordon Brown still go to church, but they do not publicly 'do' Christian supernatural doctrine at all. Quietly, they make it clear that for them (as for Clement Attlee) it is the values that count.

There used to be a popular saying that 'We are all socialists nowadays'. Still more is it true that 'We are all post-Christians nowadays'. The culture of the West goes on being Christian and goes on developing long after the death of God and the end of revealed Christian 'Truth'. It's the indelible, the feeling for life, and the human fellow feeling that count.

Notes

1 In Western Europe (unlike Eastern) there are clocks on churches, and the monk's day was from the earliest period carefully timetabled.

2 Basically secular narratives about human relationships are remarkably prominent in the Hebrew Bible and in the Apocrypha. These narratives have always been loved, and battling women are often prominent in them – Ruth, Esther, Judith, Susannah. Wives and family life also appear – Sarah, Rebekah, Rachel, Tobit and so on. This Jewish, bickering and domestic brand of humanism became very important when in the later Middle Ages Christianity at long last began to escape from the monasteries and to assert the value and interest of the domestic life of laypeople. Erich Auerbach, in *Dante: Poet of the Secular World* (New York: NYRB, 2007), saw the beginnings of modern fiction in the small narratives about everyday human life that are embedded in the cantos of the great Christian epic. Thus both in the Hebrew Bible and in Dante the old religious world-view provided the necessary cradle within which a fully modern secular selfhood could be nurtured.

3 The way Christian doctrine functions as a bridge to secular modernity is very neatly illustrated by the African experience. Nearly every African leader who emerged after 1945 was a product of the mission schools, where it was a simple version of standard Christian doctrine, and certainly not 'Greek culture', that enabled him to move from tribal culture to modernity within one lifetime. Such figures remained grateful to the mission school, even though as adults they were of course no longer literal believers. And that, in a nutshell, is where nearly all of us are today. Christian teaching in the primary school is still the ordinary person's entry ticket to modern selfhood.

4 Note the promised future disappearance of 'organized religion' (i.e. the familiar apparatus of mediation between the individual human being and God) in Jeremiah 31.33f. and Revelation 21.22.

5 See, for example, Gianni Vattimo, *Belief*, ET by Luca D'Isanto

and David Webb (Cambridge: The Polity Press, 1999); *After Christianity* (New York: Columbia University Press, 2002); and the debate with Rorty in Santiago Zabala (ed.), *The Future of Religion* (New York: Columbia University Press, 2005).

6 Thomas Clarkson was perhaps the most dedicated and hard-working of all abolitionists, and it is a shame that such a great man should have been eclipsed in the popular memory by the fame of Wilberforce. So I mention him. Go and visit his monument in Wisbech.

7 *The Philosophy of Right*, §258. See the admirably clear and sober work by Schlomo Avineri, *Hegel's Theory of the Modern State* (Cambridge: Cambridge University Press, 1972).

8 See Thomas J. J. Altizer, 'The Atheistic Ground of America', in *American Religious Empiricism: Working Papers: Vol. 1*, ed. William J. Hynes and William Dean (Weston MA: Regis College Press, 1988). This is one of the very best of all Altizer's writings, and hits the nail on the head very smartly.

9 *To the Ephesians*, 6; cf. *To the Philadelphians*, 1.

10 Matthew 5.48.

11 Leviticus 19.2.

12 Psalm 8.5 having started this train of thought.

13 Kierkegaard's phrase.

14 E. L. Mascall, an English theologian active around 1940–80, has a discussion of popes in heaven, arguably the most absurd idea ever put forward by a theologian.

15 Don Cupitt, *Radicals and the Future of the Church* (London: SCM Press, 1989), pp. 106–112.

16 There are in all five Patriarchs generally acknowledged since late antiquity: they are the bishops of Constantinople, Jerusalem, Antioch, Alexandria and Rome. The Western Patriarch, he of Rome, is not the only one to be styled 'pope': the Coptic Patriarch, he of Alexandria, is still customarily referred to as a pope.

17 The Latin Church has been 'Catholic', in the sense that the Patriarch of the West has claimed universal jurisdiction over the whole Church, since medieval times; but it is only 'Roman Catholic' when the whole world becomes a kind of extension of the diocese of Rome, using the *Missale Romanum* with the Roman martyrology, and generally following the laws and customs of the diocese of Rome in all the details of its life. In this strong sense, the Western Church as been (almost fully) *Roman* Catholic only since the nineteenth century. Those who doubt this are invited to produce pre-1830 uses by Catholics of the phrase 'the Roman Catholic Church'.

18 In this connection, note well the contribution of Ratzinger to

Joseph Ratzinger and Marcello Pera, *Without Roots: The West, Relativism, Christianity, Islam* (New York: Basic Books, 2006). In his essay Ratzinger takes an almost Catholic-fundamentalist view of the near-identity of 'the West' with 'the Roman Catholic Church'.

19 Good examples are St Thérèse of Lisieux towards the end of her life, and Mother Teresa of Calcutta for several decades of her life.

20 1 Corinthians 3.21.

21 A similar point has been made more recently by Slavoj Žižek and others. Søren Kierkegaard is another example of a philosopher and religious writer whose general account of the human situation is simultaneously very Christian *and* interesting to secular modern people.

22 Genesis 6.5 NRSV. The *yeser hara*, 'the evil imagination', was a Jewish forerunner of the later dogma of Original Sin. It may be added here that warnings about deceit, deception, the deceitfulness of the heart, and so on are very numerous throughout the Bible, and of course they imply a recommendation of constant critical vigilance.

23 In the same way, Scandinavians are very protective about their national Lutheran churches, maintaining the principal buildings immaculately, and firmly defending the establishment of the Church even though they don't believe in the faith or attend the Church's services any longer. The modern Scandinavian public is firmly *post*-Lutheran, but is also still very determinedly *Lutheran*.

24 My point here is that worldwide humanitarian concern is a very recent development, but is of Christian origin and is likely to prove indelible. It is not easy to give it up, once we have been touched by it.

25 The Augustinian tradition adds another point: the Creator of the world is also *our* creator, and he has made the world to be a home and a 'vale of soul-making' for us. Thus there was supposed to be a pre-established harmony between the human mind and the world-order, and it is this harmony that makes scientific theory possible.

26 *Vite de' piu eccellenti architetti, pittore e scultori italiani* (1550, revised edn. 1568).

27 For the distinction between heterological and autological thinking, see my *The Old Creed and the New* (London: SCM Press, 2006).

28 For example, Richard I. Aaron, *John Locke* (Oxford: Oxford University Press, 1965 edn), pp. 24–35, 292–301. When Locke is doing his 'ontotheology', he takes a notably intuitionist view of reason.

29 John Passmore, in *The Perfectibility of Man* (London: Duckworth, 1972 edn) is good on the continuities here. Western people's hopes for a future social perfection of humankind remain remarkably similar from the prophet Jeremiah to John Lennon.

30 In *The Genealogy of Morals* (1887), Nietzsche goes further and directly connects critical thinking with asceticism. Human suffering has no objective meaning, but human beings desperately need somehow to *give* it a meaning, and do so by relentlessly pursuing self-discipline, self-mortification, self-purification – in a word, self-*criticism*. See n. 28.

31 See Passmore, *The Perfectibility of Man*, especially chapters 8–10.

32 Heidegger is particularly pessimistic. For the best ET and comments, see David Farrell Krell (ed.), *Martin Heidegger: Basic Writings* (rev. and expanded edn, London: Routledge, 1993), VII, pp. 307–41.

33 As is well known, Nietzsche sees his version of nihilism – the doctrine that the world is morally neutral: there is no moral world-order and no purposiveness out there – as restoring 'the innocence of becoming'. See *Twilight of the Idols* (1888), 'The Four Great Errors', 8.

34 Albert Schweitzer, *The Quest of the Historical Jesus* (first complete edn, London: SCM Press, 2000), Chapters 21 and 25. Kafka's short story 'In the Penal Colony' expresses his reaction on reading Schweitzer's book.

35 The question here being raised was posed in the 1940s and 1950s with especial force by Sartre, and by Camus in *The Myth of Sisyphus*.

36 In Rome, many of the most ancient parish churches of the fifth to tenth centuries have been turned over to the state, which in restoring them (very well, be it said) has made clear what modest buildings they originally were. See, too, in the inscriptions of the same period preserved at St John Lateran, a standard of Latin scarcely better than we find at that time in Wales.

37 Clement of Rome, *Epistle* 1.5.

38 From the sonnet 'On The Extinction of the Venetian Republic'.

39 M. K. Gandhi's famous line to the effect that 'Western Civilization would be a very good thing' shows that people had scarcely begun to use the phrase before others were busy mocking it.

40 By W. E. Henley (1849–1903).

41 A. E. Housman, *Last Poems*, in *Collected Poems* (Harmondsworth and New York: Penguin, 1956).

42 From 'On the Prospect of Planting Arts and Learning in

America'. See A. A. Luce and T. E. Jessop (eds), *The Works of George Berkeley* (London: Nelson, 1955), vol. VII, pp. 369ff.

43 By Horace B. Greeley (1811–72).

44 I've said this before, and I say it again now, that *secular* America at its best is much more interestingly religious than is ecclesiastical America.

45 Jean Baudrillard, *Amerique* (Paris: Grasset, 1986; ET, London and New York: Verso, 1988).

46 Jean Baudrillard, *America*, trans C. Turner (London: Verso Books, 1988), pp. 90f.

47 *Paradise Lost* XII, ll.641–9.

48 After all these years, Mircea Eliade's essay, *The Myth of the Eternal Return* (New York: Bollingen Foundation, Pantheon Books, 1954), remains the best and clearest exposition of the connection between linear, historical time and the consciousness of sin.

49 Karl Löwith, in *Meaning in History* (Chicago: Chicago University Press, 1949), argued that the Western idea of progress is a secularization of Christian eschatology. Hans Blumenberg, in *The Legitimacy of the Modern Age* (1966; second edn, three vols, 1973, 1974, 1976; ET Robert M. Wallace, Cambridge MA: MIT Press, 1985), objected, making the obvious point that the realization of the Christian future depended entirely on divine intervention; whereas the realization of progress in modernity depends only upon 'immanent' human effort.

Blumenberg's argument is shallow, and shows a lack of understanding of theology. In the classical predestinarian theologies of Augustine and Calvin, the faith that God does everything motivates human beings to strive very energetically indeed to do what God wills. Because God has decreed that it will happen, you battle so hard for it, that in effect you'll make it happen anyway (even, dare I say it, if God does not exist!). So human striving and divine predestination are not alternatives; they run together, perhaps one should say 'at different levels'.

50 Baudrillard, *America* pp. 90f.

51 For English readers, James Burnett, Lord Monboddo, author of *On the Origin and Progress of Language* (6 vols, 1774–92), provided an evolutionary-historical account of human origins almost a century before Darwin. Early nineteenth-century writers often mention 'the Monboddo doctrine' – as Dickens does in the Preface to *Martin Chuzzlewit* (1843), clearly assuming that his readers are familiar with the theory.

52 Löwith, *Meaning in History*. The thesis that the philosophers of the Enlightenment were recycling traditional Christian ideas is also put forward in Carl L. Becker, *The Heavenly City of the*

Eighteenth-Century Philosophers (New Haven and London: Yale University Press, 1932).

53 Hans Blumenberg, *Die Legitimatät der Neuzeit* (Frankfurt: Suhrkamp Verlag, 1966). The translator, Robert M. Wallace, has a useful essay at the beginning of his English version, *The Legitimacy of the Modern Age*.

54 This point is emphasized by Michel de Certeau in *The Mystic Fable* (Chicago: Chicago University Press, 1992), vol. 1.

55 John Dominic Crossan, Robert W. Funk and other writers from the 'Jesus Seminar' group take this view, pointing out that the original sayings of Jesus, so far as we can reconstruct them, contain surprisingly little theology; and that the very earliest Gospels known to us seem to have been mere sayings-gospels. So the tradition of Jesus' teaching goes back to the beginning, whereas the traditions about his *life* are almost all secondary.

56 The *Diatessaron* of Tatian (*c.* AD 160) is regarded as the first harmony of the Gospels. In the Syriac Churches it was so popular that for some centuries it was regarded as the standard text of the Gospels.

57 Nathanial Culpepper's *Herbal* continued to be revised and reprinted in popular editions until the late nineteenth century, and even more recently.

58 A point made, while it was being written, by the present Pope (who may have taken it from K. R. Popper).

59 The philosophers were Hume, Paley and Schopenhauer. Darwin felt that the case for design, as presented in popular religious apologetics, was very weak and asks several correspondents to help him, by producing better arguments for design for him to combat.

60 Zanzibar was for years the headquarters of the Arab slave trade in East Africa, and building relics of slavery are still to be seen there.

61 For the 'Four Idols', see Bacon's *Novum Organum* (1620). Nowadays Descartes is regarded as the first great modern theorist of and apologist for critical thinking, and Bacon is relatively disparaged – perhaps a little unfairly.

62 Genesis 2.19f.

63 Psalm 82.6, John 10.34.

64 Luke 12.57.

65 Mark 2.27.

66 A model early Christian sermon to the Greeks is credited to St Paul in Acts 17.22–31. The surviving apologists confirm that this was indeed their procedure.

67 *Republic* VI, 509 (the Good is beyond being); VII, 514f. (language used in the Cave has a different *reference* from language used

out in the open). Read the whole argument, highlighting all allu-
sions to language.

68 Isaiah 40.18, 25; 46.5; etc. For the divine darkness, see Psalm
18.11 and, in general, in the Bible remember to make a clear distinction between human moral darkness caused by sin, and the deep,
'dazzling', epistemological darkness in which God is hidden.

69 See n. 67 above.

70 Jacques Derrida, *Writing and Difference*, trans. Alan Bass
(London: Routledge, 1978), p. 146: The negative theology 'is only a
phase of positive ontotheology'. Here Derrida nods.

71 2 Corinthians 5.4.

72 The patristic scholar G. C. Stead has made this point in a
well-known paper. Note a curious point in Christian iconography:
the damned in hell do look different from each other; but the re-
deemed in heaven are all clones, quite indistinguishable except by
their sex.

73 Revelation 7.4.

74 Most of them are to be found in Aquinas. Even sillier arguments are to be found in other apologists, like the one who argued
for the benevolence of God from the sweet smell of the dung of
horses. God foresaw that many ploughmen and coachmen would
have to spend their lives behind horses, so he designed the horse
with sweet-smelling dung. Intelligent design, indeed.

75 In this connection note the rise of allegory as a literary form
in Latin antiquity.

76 See above, p. 38.

77 'Work out your own salvation with fear and trembling ...',
Philippians 2.12. That the believer's first concern should be for his
or her own salvation has remained orthodox Roman Catholic doctrine, and was reaffirmed at the Council of Trent against those who
in various ways have taught what might be called 'ecstatic self-
denial', or pure love.

78 See Chapter 4 above.

79 The undivided Church defined only the dogmas of the Incarnation and the Trinity. It is certainly arguable that God, the atoning
work of Christ, the resurrection, the ascension (i.e. strictly, the
heavenly session) of Christ, and the doctrine of Man remain largely
undefined. So is much else, but many people pretend otherwise.

80 Mark 2.27. The whole passage has attracted a great deal of
comment. See, for example, Robert W. Funk, Roy W. Hoover and
others, *The Five Gospels* (New York: Scribner, 1996), pp. 49f.

81 The biblical 'dream' resurfaced very strongly in the America
of the 1960s, most famously in Martin Luther King's famous speech,
and in John Lennon's popular song of the early 1970s, 'Imagine'.

82 1 Kings 4.25.

83 Psalm 128.3.

84 Psalm 128.6.

85 Revelation 6.1–8, but the whole passage is somewhat vague, it must be confessed.

86 I refer here especially to the many writings of John Dominic Crossan and other members of the Jesus Seminar, mentioned in notes 55 and 80, above. For example, Crossan, *Jesus: A Revolutionary Biography* (New York: HarperCollins, 1994).

87 Thomas L. Thompson, *The Bible in History: How Writers Create a Past* (London: Jonathan Cape, 1999), is one of the first writers to state the (obviously correct) view that the entire history recounted in the Hebrew Bible is an edifying romance about an imagined national past, which may incorporate some scraps of old traditions. Those who angrily reject Thompson's views must persuade their friends the biblical archaeologists to produce the coins of the pre-exilic kings of Israel and Judah. Until that is done, we should presume that Thompson is right.

88 The last of these seven, well known to be a standard religious duty for all Jews and Muslims, has been added here merely in order to make up the number. It could hardly have been attributed to Jesus, in view of Matthew 8.21f.

89 Acts 6.1–6.

90 Sir Thomas Browne says this explicitly in his *Religio Medici* (1642). He is very definitely *not* a humanitarian: 'I give no alms to satisfy the hunger of my brother, but to fulfil and accomplish the will and command of my God' (Part Two, Section II). On the other hand, one could plausibly claim that Jonathan Swift and John Locke, each in his own odd way, *were* humanitarians. Childless, they liked children, and *felt for* people very different from themselves, which brings them close to the great and ever-memorable Thomas Coram (1688–1751). Perhaps it was the increasing coldness of the new mechanistic universe that drove people more and more to value human warmth and fellow feeling.

91 William Wordsworth, *The Prelude* (1805), III, 59. The line refers to the statue in the antechapel at Trinity College. The losers, the Cambridge Platonists Whichcote, Culverwell, Cudworth, Smith and Peter Sterry were, by the way, graduates of my own College, Emmanuel.

92 In Britain, the Society for the Prevention of Cruelty to Animals is *Royal*, and the Society for the Prevention of Cruelty to Children remains merely *National*, no doubt because the highest social class in England have always been very much kinder to their animals than to their unfortunate children.

93 It is worth stressing, by the way, that Beveridge was a Liberal and not a Socialist. He insisted that social provision must complement, and not replace, individual initiative.

94 I am referring especially, of course, to David Hume and to J.-J. Rousseau. Hume's philosophy is in many ways close to Nietzsche's.

95 Heidegger surely never read William James and John Dewey. But from *Being and Time* onwards Heidegger's reconstruction of the theory of knowledge has a marked resemblance to pragmatism.

96 A line from the early Nietzsche, who was pushed towards pragmatism by his early encounter with Darwin.

97 See my earlier comments (nn. 55 and 80) on the work of John Dominic Crossan and other members of the Jesus Seminar. Without getting too involved in critical questions, there is a very brief reminder of the original Jesus' secular religion of commitment to life and transience in Matthew 6.22—7.14.

98 See 1 Corinthians 16.22.

Bibliography

This booklist includes modern (i.e. post-Enlightenment) works expressly quoted and referred to in the Notes, and a few other works alluded to in the main text.

Aaron, Richard I., *John Locke*, Oxford: Oxford University Press, 1965 edn.

Auerbach, Erich, *Dante: Poet of the Secular World*, Introduction by Michael Dirda, New York: NYRB, 2007.

Avineri, Schlomo, *Hegel's Theory of the Modern State*, Cambridge: Cambridge University Press, 1972.

Baudrillard, Jean, *Amerique*, Paris: Grasset, 1986; ET, London and New York: Verso, 1988.

Becker, Carl L., *The Heavenly City of the Eighteenth Century Philosophers*, New Haven and London: Yale University Press, 1932.

Blumenberg, Hans, *The Legitimacy of the Modern Age*, ET Robert M. Wallace, Cambridge MA: MIT Press, 1985. (See also the Introduction by Wallace.)

Burnett, James (= Lord Monboddo), *On the Origin and Progress of Language*, 6 vols, 1774–92.

Burns, Robert M. and Rayment-Pickard, Hugh, *Philosophies of History: Enlightenment to Postmodernity*, Malden MA and Oxford: Blackwell, 2000.

Conrad, Peter, *Creation: Artists, Gods and Origins*, London: Thames & Hudson, 2007.

Crossan, John Dominic, *Jesus: A Revolutionary Biography*, New York: HarperCollins, 1994.

Cupitt, Don, *Radicals and the Future of the Church*, London: SCM Press, 1989.

Cupitt, Don, *The Old Creed and the New*, London: SCM Press, 2006.

Derrida, Jacques, *Writing and Difference*, ET Alan Bass, London and New York: Routledge, 1978.

Eliade, Mircea, *The Myth of the Eternal Return*, New York: Bollingen Foundation, Pantheon Books, 1954.

Funk, Robert W., Hoover, Roy and Others, *The Five Gospels*, New York: Scribner, 1996.

Gill, Stephen, ed., *William Wordsworth: The Major Works*, New York and Oxford: Oxford University Press, 2000 (World's Classics Paperback). (The poems in chronological order, and in their earliest completed versions.)

Guignon, Charles, ed., *The Cambridge Companion to Heidegger*, New York and Cambridge: Cambridge University Press, 1993. (See essay 10, by John D. Caputo.)

Heidegger, Martin, *Being and Time*, ET John Macquarrie and Edward Robinson, Oxford: Basil Blackwell, 1962.

Housman, A. E., *Collected Poems*, Penguin Poetry Library, Harmondsworth and New York, 1956. (See *Last Poems*, I, 'The West'.)

Hynes, William J. and Dean, William (eds), *American Religious Empiricism: Working Papers: Vol. 1*, Weston MA: Regis College Press, 1988. (Contribution by Altizer.)

Kafka, Franz, *The Short Stories*, Oxford: Oxford University Press, 1977.

Krell, David Farrell (ed.), *Martin Heidegger: Basic Writings*, London: Routledge, rev. and expanded edn., 1993.

Kuhn, Thomas S., *The Structure of Scientific Revolutions*, Chicago: Chicago University Press, 1962.

Löwith, Karl, *Meaning in History*, Chicago: Chicago University Press, 1949.

Luce, A. A. and Jessop, T. E. (eds), *The Works of George Berkeley*, vol. VII, London: Nelson, 1955. (For Berkeley's minor writings, including verse.)

Nietzsche, Friedrich, *The Genealogy of Morals*, 1887.

Nietzsche, Friedrich, *Twilight of the Idols*, 1888. (The translations by R. J. Hollingdale are recommended.)

Otto, Rudolf, *The Idea of the Holy*, ET London: Methuen, 1923.

Passmore, John, *The Perfectibility of Man*, London: Duckworth, 1972 edn.

Ratzinger, Joseph and Pera, Marcello, *Without Roots: The West, Relativism, Christianity, Islam*, New York: Basic Books, 2006.

Schweitzer, Albert, *The Quest of the Historical Jesus*, first complete edn, London: SCM Press, 2000. (A translation, edited by John Bowden, of the 1913 German edition.)

Thompson, Thomas L., *The Bible in History: How Writers Create a Past*, London: Jonathan Cape, 1999.

Vasari, Giorgio, *Vite de' piu eccellenti architetti, pittore e scultori italiani*, 1550, rev. edn, 1568.

Vattimo, Gianni, *Belief*, ET Luca D'Isanto and David Webb, Cambridge: The Polity Press, 1999.

Zabala, Santiago (ed.), *The Future of Religion*, New York: Columbia University Press, 2005. (Contributions by Vattimo and Rorty.)

Žižek, Slavoj, *The Fragile Absolute: Or, Why is the Christian Legacy Worth Fighting For?* London and New York: Verso, 2000.

Index